Beat Till Stiff

A Woman's Recipe for Living

Beat Till Stiff

A Woman's Recipe for Living

Peta Mathias

PENGUIN BOOKS

Published by the Penguin Group

Penguin Group (NZ), 67 Apollo Drive, Rosedale,
Auckland 0632, New Zealand (a division of Pearson New Zealand Ltd)

Penguin Group (USA) Inc., 375 Hudson Street,
New York, New York 10014, USA

Penguin Group (Canada), 90 Eglinton Avenue East, Suite 700, Toronto,
Ontario, M4P 2Y3, Canada (a division of Pearson Penguin Canada Inc.)

Penguin Books Ltd, 80 Strand, London, WC2R 0RL, England

Penguin Ireland, 25 St Stephen's Green,
Dublin 2, Ireland (a division of Penguin Books Ltd)

Penguin Group (Australia), 250 Camberwell Road, Camberwell,
Victoria 3124, Australia (a division of Pearson Australia Group Pty Ltd)

Penguin Books India Pvt Ltd, 11, Community Centre,
Panchsheel Park, New Delhi – 110 017, India

Penguin Books (South Africa) (Pty) Ltd, 24 Sturdee Avenue,
Rosebank, Johannesburg 2196, South Africa

Penguin Books Ltd, Registered Offices: 80 Strand,
London, WC2R 0RL, England

First published by Penguin Group (NZ), 2011
1 3 5 7 9 10 8 6 4 2

Copyright © Peta Mathias, 2011

The right of Peta Mathias to be identified as the author of this work in terms of
section 96 of the Copyright Act 1994 is hereby asserted.

Designed, illustrated and typeset by Sarah Healey, © Penguin Group (NZ)
Typeset in Chaparral Pro 11/15pt
Printed in Australia by McPherson's Printing Group

ISBN 978 014 356670 0

A catalogue record for this book is available
from the National Library of New Zealand.

www.penguin.co.nz

Contents

Introduction

We must be willing to get rid of the life we've planned so as to have the life that is waiting for us.

Joseph Campbell

When I told my publisher I wanted to call my book on women 'Beat Till Stiff', they screamed and fell on the floor. When I told them I wanted to call my book on men 'Beat Till Stiff', they smiled indulgently. So when I wanted to call a book on transformation 'Beat Till Stiff', they gave in. 'Beat till stiff' is a culinary term to describe whipping egg whites and 'a recipe for living' is a tongue-in-cheek take on transformation stories. I have always been fascinated by events in life where something changes into something else following the simple introduction of a transforming element. With egg whites, it was the introduction of a whisk; with Edith Piaf, it was the day she met her first impresario; with tattooing, it was the discovery that if you make a hole in skin and rub ash into it, the blue colour will stay there forever.

In this book, I talk about topics that I find interesting or important. The first of these begs the question: why do redheads have more fun? The association of redheads with temptation and provocation is, it seems, something entirely invented by men, mostly because genuine red hair is unusual – only 2 per cent of the world's population have it. In this chapter, I look into the history of red hair and how it happened in the first place; and also the history of the colour red and how it changed the world.

Needless to say, there is also an essay on my favourite topic, sex – surely one of the most transformative activities in the world. An orgasm is wonderful and briefly puts you in another world. So why do women have multiple orgasms and not men? We don't need to have one to get pregnant, so what is the genetic purpose of multiple orgasms? Are they evolutionary or are they a mistake? Does having even one orgasm really make any difference to sex, procreation or world peace?

In the essay entitled 'Eat, Sing, Love', I discuss the transformative power of food, music and romance. In this semi-autobiographical chapter you'll find out what it means to go picking strawberries with a man in the south-west of France, and how music transforms and unites.

But before you fall in love, you have to stop strangling your mother. Some women have difficult relationships with their mothers – as it turns out, this is not particularly original or different. Most mothers and daughters have ongoing tugs of war that start right from birth. The first snaps of anger appear as young as eight months and are an ordinary part of development. Living with my mother was like living in a game show, which could be exciting sometimes – but one false move could make you lose thousands. When I grew up, I found out that blaming your mother keeps you passive and dependent, and unable to take responsibility for your own transformation.

In the chapter called 'How to Buy Hope' you will find out about the transformative power (or not) of face cream. It seems to me that growing older is mostly maintenance and cheating, preventing the rot leading to our inevitable fate. Life is just one goddamn thing after another – you do all that work, you slap on all that moisturiser and then you don't even get out of it alive. It's the dance of keeping up appearances but as it happens, you don't have to spend a lot of money on it – whiskey and Nivea will do the job just as well as face lifts and La Mer.

Quite aside from face cream, I wish I had known a lot of things, which is why I wrote a letter to my much younger self, giving advice on where my performance could have improved. As I wrote this essay, it made me weep to think of all the years I wasted being a nurse and a counsellor and a cook in the hot, hard kitchens of the world. My missionary complex unfortunately obliterated the abilities I was born with: entertaining and drama. It wasn't until I was forty-five that I finally became who I was supposed to be: a writer and television presenter. Talk about slow transformation!

In the 1970s everyone was into transformation as a lifestyle, and if you weren't in therapy or an encounter group you were a loser, unwilling to 'work on yourself'. In the essay on my brush with mental illness, I explain how transformation can go very wrong. It turns out that screaming doesn't bring about change. I actually invented Primal Scream but some American guy took all the credit. I started screaming at the pepper tree in my childhood garden to stop me from strangling my mother long before Arthur Janov came along. I became a therapist in a treatment centre in Quebec for drug addicts and alcoholics and learned how to confuse transformation with destruction.

The essays in *Beat Till Stiff* don't have grey areas – they are pungent, sometimes scurrilous, sometimes sad, sometimes funny, sometimes grim and sometimes autobiographical. What did I learn from writing this book? That time passes and transformation happens anyway.

Why Redheads Have More Fun

Out of the ash
I rise with my red hair
And eat men like air.

From 'Lady Lazarus' by Sylvia Plath

The history of red hair

In my kitchen cupboard there's a bottle of XXX-rated chilli sauce with a name only a man could invent – *Pleasure & Pain*. Helpful information on the bottle includes 'It Hurts So Good' and 'You've Got To Have It'. Gracing the label is a voluptuous redhead wearing a black leather bikini, thigh-high leather boots and black gloves. She's flashing a licentious smile and holding a whip. Any association between redheads, temptation and provocation is entirely invented by men, mostly because red hair is unusual –

only 2 per cent of the world's population have it. Also at play here is the fact that eating chilli is very much a boy activity involving scatological jokes, sexual innuendo and sometimes taking place at embarrassing 'heat geek' festivals. There, men discuss SHU ratings (the measure of chilli hotness) and wank on about the latest harvest from Outer Mongolia and Bangladesh.

When you eat really hot chilli, your body reacts strongly. Neurotransmitters inside the brain scream, telling it an assault has occurred and you have to cool your body down. This causes you to sweat, your nose runs, eyes weep and endorphins race around in your blood. And this is exactly what happens when a man comes into contact with a redheaded woman – he perspires, his teeth hurt and he thinks he's stoned.

Red is the colour of life – if you are afraid of red, you are afraid of life. So, in the recipe for good living, if you don't have red, get with it. It is also the colour of both danger and sexual arousal. Men think redheads are going to be fiery all over, trembling tabernacles of passion and unpredictability, possibly witches with trick pelvises at best, and pocket rockets at worst.

There are two real auburns among my five brothers and sisters – and one faux. It has always been said that redheads have hot tempers and acidic tongues. I suspect redheads became temperamental not because it is inherent in their nature, but because they have suffered so much abuse and teasing. In the fifteenth century, Germans tortured and murdered 45,000 red-haired women; Greeks believed redheads became vampires upon death; Egyptians burned them alive. Folk have picked on redheads ever since. Every single fireball I interviewed for this story said they had been tormented as children, called tarty, a freak of nature, ginga, blue, Duracell, carrot-top, et cetera. In my parents' day the most incendiary redhead of all was Maureen O'Hara, who spent a lot of time throwing tantrums and bossing John Wayne around. In the past, redheads were thought of as being sexually degenerate and morally suspect. Some people also maintain they smell different. My red-haired brother and sister are spectacularly even-tempered, don't possess an eighth of the sarcasm or sharp tongue I do, are not sex maniacs and smell the same as everyone else. In fact, I don't think I've ever met a hysterical redhead, but I have met a lot of redheads who love attention and are flamboyant.

When my sister was born we all crowded around the bed the day my mother brought her home. I was a dark brunette, my brother David was a strawberry blond, my brother Jonathan had brown hair and here was this unbearably beautiful baby with blue eyes and copper hair. I realised then that all my brothers and sisters were going to have different-coloured hair and admired my parents' cleverness at orchestrating this. Pretty soon Keriann's newborn hair turned into adorable, thick curls, like caramel flowing around her head. It was like having a movie-star baby – everywhere we went with our 'mascot', people gushed at her prettiness, plumpness and redness. To cap it all off, she had little rosebud lips and an easy-to-get-along-with personality, in stark contrast to her elder, high-maintenance sister who was blessed with the character of car paint – tough and hard-wearing. When she grew up, Keriann had darker, madder-coloured hair in huge wavy curls, pink cupid lips and cerulean eyes.

• • •

So what does a true redhead look like apart from the fireball on her scalp? Well, remarkably like she did 40,000-odd years ago actually, because the human genetic code is quite strident. She *looks* Celtic, and if she is from an unbroken Celtic line, is probably heart-stoppingly beautiful with refined features. She has pale skin, which can vary from deathly white to freckled to fair-but-capable-of-a-tan. She has a high patrician forehead with elegant eyebrows, a fine tapered nose, a firm but not prominent chin and thin lips. People often remark on the softness of a redhead's eyes, which are usually grey, blue or green. One of the most stunning combinations is red hair with brown eyes, which is quite unusual because the brown eyes came from somewhere else.

It is common to think of people with russet hair and blue eyes as Irish. In fact, it is more likely that they have Scottish blood. The most common form of Irish beauty is actually black hair and green or dark brown eyes. Technically, red hair is a genetic mutation only seen in Celts. Thirteen per cent of Scots have red hair and 40 per cent carry the recessive red gene, as opposed to the Irish with 10 per cent ginger and 30 per cent carrying the gene. Scientists at the Oxford Hair Foundation say red hair will eventually disappear, and quite soon – maybe even by 2100. This is a lie put about by blond scientists. The single gene that causes red hair is called MCIR, but it has many variations and mutations, all of which are code for different colours. How did this happen in our genetic history, and when? It's an entirely Celtic northern European thing, and like all skin and hair colour, the mutation was a reaction to sunlight. Being red-haired and having this weird gene increased a person's ability to deal with the sun without suffering too much damage. And it enabled the person to make vitamin D from sunlight.

This gene enjoyed high currency when there were lots of redheads and they were all mating with each other. But time passed and they began breeding with other people who didn't have the gene (brunettes and blonds). This weakened the powerful protective MCIR gene and today's redheads are susceptible to heat, burning, skin cancer, extreme hot and cold and are more sensitive to pain. If you operate on a redhead, you need to use 20 per cent more anaesthetic than on, say, a brunette. A redhead can make a red-haired baby with a person of a different hair colour, but they have much more chance of producing a redhead if they have a naturally red-haired partner. On the other hand, my brother and sister were produced by a brunette mother and blond father with no obvious history of redheads in the family. Those children have not produced any redheads, but their children or grandchildren might because the gene can rest unexpressed for generations before springing up again.

● ● ●

Some people think blondes have more fun. Hello? I don't think so. Here's why men like blondes, and it's not pretty. Have you noticed that a man will eat a chair to impress a blonde? The theory is that because most white babies are born fair, we all instinctively view the adult versions as adorable, tiny-minded infants who need protecting for their own good. This is why white men think blondes are dumb. But white men are dumb anyway, so what do black men think? They like redheads because they like contrast – they like fiery. When a man meets a blonde he perceives her as having a low IQ. This is a trick on the blonde's part – the man acts like an idiot in her presence because he hopes she will drop her high IQ long enough to make the mistake of falling for him. A brief aside: women with hourglass figures – small waists and big hips – are the ideal mate because they live longer, are more intelligent and are sexier. This is all due to large deposits of omega-3 fatty acids on their thighs and bottoms. So there it is, men – if you want the perfect woman who is hot in the sack, has translucent skin, produces top-quality babies and will always be exciting, choose a curvy redhead.

• • •

There is a sub-species called the faux redhead – those who dye their hair red. For years being around my redheaded brother and sister, I failed to realise I was a closet redhead. What helped the closet door to creak open was when my grey hair situation finally came to a head (sorry). I had been going grey since I was seventeen and ignoring it. The years went by and I embraced being a naturally grey brunette, then one night I was at a black dance club in Paris with my youngest sister, fifteen years my junior. I was in my early forties, all the guys were asking her to dance and I got to be the salt and pepper ugly sister, alone on the barstool, weeping into my piña colada. Finally some guy said to Desirée, 'Doesn't your mother want to dance?' She laughed and I cried. The next day I went and bought some red hair dye and drowned myself in it – I haven't seen my hair since and no longer have any idea what colour it is. The really interesting thing is that I have fair skin, freckles and hazel eyes, so I suited red hair well. It took all of five minutes for my friends to forget I was a greying brunette. (Did you know you have all the freckles you are ever going to have by the time you are fifteen?) Once in my redhead life, I dyed my hair back to its natural dark brown. For one month. The reaction from my colleagues and friends was the same as if I had undergone chemotherapy for fun: 'Why would you do that? You look frightening. Go back to your "natural" red hair right now.'

• • •

Here's how it feels to be a brunette: like everyone else. Here's how it feels to be a redhead: attractive, alive, spreading light and fireworks everywhere, impossible to ever look old and dowdy. The thing about getting older is that colour drains out of you, and having red hair and red lips brings colour back in without the need for major make-up, needles or screaming to bring the blood up to the cheeks. Nobody's fooled when a middle-aged woman has fire-engine red hair – but they do think she is having fun and is beyond worrying what people think of her.

Warning! Only dye your hair red if it will suit your skin – olive-skinned people generally look terrible with red hair. Of course there is a bizarre school of thought that suggests you should accept your birth hair colour gracefully, be at one with the universe, get your priorities straight, eschew vanity. Give me a break. I can't stand people who say that – don't they have a mirror? Or do they think mouse is a colour? Another thing: natural red hair fades as quickly as dyed red hair, so it's a lot of work to keep that light shining – it takes commitment. Faded red hair with a centimetre of mouse is a cry for help and God's way of telling you that you are taking too much Prozac. Women who run with the mice are missing the spice.

The downside to red hair is it attracts a lot of attention – it can be seen from the other side of the harbour. You can never hide and sometimes it feels as if you are wearing a miner's light on your head. When you get sick of the loudness of it, think of the alternative – it cures you instantly.

Commitment to red

This is what I mean by commitment. Being a faux red-haired travel writer means you wander around the world showing nonplussed hairdressers a piece of paper with the recipe for your colour on it. The worst experience I had was in Hué, Vietnam. My hair needed seeing to; it had been a month since I had darkened the doors of a salon and I felt if I could survive the Vietnamese dress makers, I could survive the hairdresser. My photographer Tanah looked nervous, but was staying open to the idea in the interests of research. We strolled across to the new town on our daring mission and discovered that the hairdressing joints in the big hotels required appointments. I, however, was into instant gratification and happy to manage all the risks resulting from such a personality flaw, so after traipsing to three recommended places, we ended up at a salon down by the river. What followed was a truly terrifying cultural experience. Never mind the risk of snakes, typhoid and malaria – get your hair coloured at a local, tin-pot salon in Vietnam. Obviously minimal English was spoken and why wouldn't it be? I showed them the L'Oréal recipe my hairdresser at home had carefully written in my diary.

'Okay. Okay madame. We no have L'Oréal but no problem. Sit down, sit down.'

I sat down and a boy jumped on a bike and raced off down the street.

'You want hand massage? You frien' want hand massage?'

'No. No thank you.'

I then received a hand massage.

'You want face massage, madame?'

'No thank you. I want my hair done.' Ten-second pause. 'Okay. I'll have a face massage.'

Every muscle in my face was rapidly and brusquely rearranged. In the middle of it, aforementioned boy arrived back from his bike dash and excitedly presented me with some products I had never heard of.

'Thank you very much but this is not L'Oréal.'

'No L'Oréal, madame. Only this.'

Tanah was looking at me with saucer eyes. 'Peta, I can't believe you're going to do this.'

'I know I might end up with black and orange hair at best, but this is a cultural experience, Tanah. It's me and the people.'

'Christ.'

'Why don't you have your hair done too?'

'Are you kidding? I'm going for a walk.'

I was thinking thoughts like, *My hair is one of the trademarks of my television food show; can my identity take ruined hair? Do I care and what does it have to do with world peace?* Bush was talking about blowing the daylights out of Iraq and I was worried about the risk of a bad hair day. I asked the staff (boys and girls basically) for their colour charts. I was given one small chart with a dozen colours on it and that was it; that was the choice. So between me, them and anyone else who walked by, we decided on my colour mixture. Bizarrely, they insisted on washing and drying my hair first. Then a boy and girl worked on me, one either side with four others giving advice. The boy on the left did a hatchet job and the girl on the right carefully isolated every single strand of the blonde streak and tied it up in a little knot. In a complete absence of method, they painted on a bright orange paste, which reeked of ammonia, ignoring the roots – till I pointed them out. They then walked away very happy with their work.

'What about the blonde bit?'

'Later, madame.'

'No. Now please.' I had visions of still being there the next day.

Someone found a plastic supermarket bag, tied it around my scalp, cut a hole in the top and pulled the blonde bit through. Tanah walked in as they were applying powder-blue paste and screamed.

'Oh my God. Where's my camera . . . where's my camera . . . tell them to wait till I focus . . . this is the front cover of the book.'

One of the boys picked up the brush with leftover blue paste on it and combed it into his black hair. A light went on in my traumatised brain and I realised the dye would be for Asian hair, which is completely different from European hair. By then I was convinced the blue would make my hair fall out and the orange would be purple, so I asked them to wash it out, which they did with conditioner, not shampoo. At this very moment the electricity cut out, which happens often in the monsoon rain, so no hair dryer would work. I haggled over the price and finally agreed on US$20, which was far too much. This whole episode took two and a half hours. If I had stayed for styling, they would have had to bring in my dinner and a bed to which I would also have had to be tied to restrain me. As aggression and hunger are closely related in the brain, rather than screaming I felt an overwhelming need to eat. The next scene saw me eating in a restaurant with red dye streaming down my white blouse.

Red in nature

There is one other redhead in the world and that is a television filming lamp. The name of my production company is Red Head Media Group – not only because I have red hair, but also after this lamp. A redhead lamp is an open-faced light used for back-lighting. There is no lens, but a light source or bubble that sits in front of a reflector. They are a good source of soft light when 'bounced' off a light surface, such as a wall or ceiling. Red light is produced by long wavelengths of light. Infrared light is even longer and is invisible to the human eye. DVDs use red lasers.

It is red wavelengths that produce a red sky in the evening and morning. At these times of the day the sun is very low in the sky and the rays must penetrate the densest part of the atmosphere. Red wavelengths are so long that they travel through the atmosphere in one piece. Clouds turn pink because, heavy with moisture, they are reflecting the red. Red clouds in the evening are travelling west, reflecting the sun setting in the west, which usually means a good day will follow. Red clouds in the morning are travelling east with the rising red wavelengths. They are heavy with moisture and this usually means it will rain.

The colour red in nature (autumn leaves, fruit, et cetera) is created by the carotene pigment, necessary for photosynthesis. Carotene only exists in plants, but animals can keep it in their bodies – it's what makes fat yellow.

The earthy red and mustard-coloured houses in Provence come from one of its most important products – the mining and treatment of ochre. This iron ore is a mixture of argillaceous sand and iron oxide which, after washing, filtering and drying, is cut into blocks. Once dried, the blocks are crushed and again sifted and sometimes baked to deepen the colour to give that orangey-red look. The red village of Roussillon-en-Provence is designated one of the most beautiful in France. And it really is red – the soil, the trees, the earth, the hills, the houses – everything is turned red by the ochre vein this village sits on. Roussillon is like a magic fairyland where seventeen different shades of red ochre tint every house, alleyway, winding stairway and ancient gateway. In spite of it being very tourist-ridden it must be the most breathtaking village I've ever seen – like a painter's palette, a sunset in stone, a village drenched in blushing passion. As you walk through amber, saffron, magenta, gold, red, pink, rust and coral, you can't help but gasp at one of the few examples of mankind building in perfect harmony with nature. The ochre quarry is called falaises d'or et de sang (cliffs of gold and blood). The mythological explanation for the colour is much more exciting than the technical one. The blood that stained Roussillon came from a woman's broken heart. In grief she threw herself from the top of the castle and the ground below was forever stained with her blood. They did that a lot in those days – there are screeds of medieval stories of barbaric love triangles and for some reason the woman always jumps off the ramparts as a problem-solving device. They don't seem to have considered counselling in their life challenges.

Red in culture

The thing about the colour red is that you can't ignore it with its ambition, power, need for attention and desire to impose itself on all other colours. The colour red has a very violent past full of sin, war, bloodshed, fire, anger and crime. Red is fascinating and charismatic, but also duplicitous, insolent and deceitful and it will burn you as soon as look at you.

Red is subversive, especially in clothing. As a nursing student I wore forbidden red petticoats under my starchy white uniforms to remind myself how stifling I found the conservative nursing hierarchy. This brings me to the only lipstick colour that counts – Simply Red. If it was good enough for Cleopatra, Elizabeth I, Elizabeth Arden, Coco Chanel and Marilyn Monroe, it's good enough for everyone. Redheads were always told not to wear red lipstick or red clothes, but I disagree. I think this sparkling combination is fantastic. The paler your skin, the better red lipstick looks. The second you apply red lipstick your face is pulled together, every other good feature is noticeable, you don't need any other make-up and you feel energised. Men are more attracted to women who wear red also, possibly because red is less frequently seen in nature, unlike green (plants) and blue (sky), and therefore is more obvious. This is why red is used in danger and warning signs.

In history red symbolises both death and life. In some African countries where it means death it isn't considered attractive. The first North American Indians that Europeans saw, loved the colour red and covered their skin, hair, clothing, possessions, friends and even dead bodies with red ochre. They mixed the red iron oxide with animal fat and rubbed it on anything that moved, which is why they were called 'redskins'. As it turned out they were neither Indian nor did they have red skin, but they looked scarily sensational.

Bulls in the bullfighting corrida are supposed to be driven mad by the colour red, but in fact they are driven mad by anything or anyone who is annoying them. It was thought toreadors flashed a red (in fact it is crimson-pink) cape to make the bull angry, but bulls are colour-blind. The other reason they used red capes was to cover the blood. But look, I've seen lots of bullfights and there's no hiding the blood! The real answer to the red cape is just that it is a traditional colour – the bull only attacks it because and when it moves.

Red succeeded in taking over the entire Orient – Chinese red or vermillion being the most dramatic shade of orange-crimson-red in existence. Chinese red is made from the mineral cinnabar and is used in making art, lacquer, furniture and fabric. It is considered the colour of life and eternity. In Europe fashionable wedding dresses were scarlet up until the fourteenth century, when the colour became associated with whores (a scarlet woman was originally just a woman who wore red), so the dresses changed to white to symbolise purity and virginity. But to this day many cultures wear red on their wedding day – the Northern Chinese, Northern Indians, Palestinians, Kazakhstani and Vietnamese. Red is considered lucky and auspicious. Japanese brides wear a red kimono which is also lined with red material – it means happiness and signals new beginnings. On my wedding day I wore a black dress with a red veil, which symbolised absolutely nothing except rebellion.

Red clothing used only to be worn by rich people and top-echelon clergy, because it was so expensive to make the dye. When I say clergy, I mean Catholics. The reforming Protestants considered red the colour of 'papists' and it was therefore immoral. In the sixteenth century you didn't see people dressed in red much unless they were cardinals. Women were more likely to wear blue, symbolising the Virgin Mary; men who wore red were associated with power and war. Then it changed, and red or pink became feminine colours and blue became masculine, which endures to this day with baby boys being dressed in blue and girls in pink.

A history of the colour red

When I was in Bolivia and Mexico, I saw peasants dyeing woollen fabric with cochineal, which is an insect. They ground the dried bodies (grana fina) till they released a rich, crimson dye. What makes these insects red is the carminic acid they produce to scare off predators. Cochineal is the most fantastic quality dye for fabric and cosmetics, because it doesn't fade, is stable when heated and is completely safe. Obviously it doesn't stay fast all by itself – it has to be fixed with metal salts like astringent alum. Nineteenth-century painters who didn't believe cochineal would fade with light found themselves in trouble with their clients because their searing red sunsets were soon pallid. Eventually the use of cochineal and crimson (made from the kermes insect which lives on the scarlet oak) went downhill in the nineteenth century with the invention of synthetic dyes such as alizarin, but now everyone is nervous about carcinogenic artificial food additives, and natural cochineal production is becoming popular again. Today it is mostly used to tint lipsticks, blusher, eye shadow, fabric, oil paints, some foodstuffs and soft drinks (E120). In the Middle Ages you had to get a permit to dye certain colours. Dyeing businesses got different licences for red garance (or madder, which is extracted from the roots of the rubia tree) and red kermes, which also permitted white and yellow. Others got licences for blue, which included green and black, et cetera. Woe betide anyone straying from their colour. The blue and red dyers had to be on separate streets in separate suburbs but still got into fights, accusing each other of polluting the rivers.

Originally produced for dyeing fabric by the Incas

and Aztecs and discovered by European travellers in the fifteenth century, the best cochineal these days still comes from Chile and Peru. The cochineal insect is a tiny, whitish, oval creature that lives on prickly pear cactus plants and basically eats them alive. If nature is left to itself the cochineal will kill the plant. It is an extraordinary sight – cactus leaves are huge, and when they are infested with the bug, look like they are covered in white powder. If you pick one bug off and squeeze it hard, deep red comes out. In the deliberate cultivation of cochineal, the plants are manually infested with pregnant bugs, left for five months, harvested, and then the cactus is re-infested three months later, after a short break. You collect the cochineal from the plants by blowing them off into buckets with compressors. In the old days the Indians brushed them off with deer tails. It's like watching people pick grapes in a vineyard – they move along the rows, dressed in protective gear, patiently collecting their live, ghostly harvest. When you've collected lots of cochineals, you kill them with heat – boiling, drying in the sun, steaming or baking in the oven. It takes 70,000 bugs to make 500 grams of dye. There is something morbid about the fact that the most beautiful shade of red in the world is the result of murdering thousands of lady insects to get their blood.

The female bugs are larger, rounder, flatter and live longer than the males, which are weedy by comparison – they are slimmer, longer, have wings and die of exhaustion after a few days of buzzing around fertilising the females. This is so often the plight of the male in nature – they die terrible deaths at the hands of or in the service of females. The praying mantis is the best-known example: the female eats the male as soon as mating is done, starting with his head. In fact sometimes she is so hungry, she actually starts cannibalising him while they are still mating. Even with his head gone, he is still alive and struggling to get away from her depraved embrace. Lots of spider species indulge in sexual cannibalisation – in fact sometimes a virgin spider tucks into her suitor before he even gets his eight legs over, if his courtship is too fast, not energetic enough, or he is a wimp. She gets cross, which seems counter-productive to me, but it does prove that women often prefer a good meal to sex.

Little Red Riding Hood

In the fairytale 'Little Red Riding Hood', the good girl goes into the forest to visit her sick grandmother, who is bed-ridden. She is wearing a red cape and carrying a cake. In the forest she meets the Big Bad Wolf, who charms her into telling him where she is going. He sneaks off to the grandmother's house ahead of her, locks Grandmother in a cupboard, dresses in her clothes and hops into her bed to wait for the little girl in the red cloak. When Little Red Riding Hood arrives she exclaims at what big teeth her grandmother has. The wolf tries to persuade her to get into bed with him. At that moment a passing woodsman walks in, saves the girl and kills the wolf. This is the sanitised version. These ghastly fairytales we feasted on as children were much loved. The violence, abuse and perversion was music to our little ears – we thought it enchanting and didn't make the mistake of confusing these stories with real life.

It is at the point when the girl arrives at her grandmother's house that the story goes in various directions, depending on the era and the person telling it. I like the version that goes like this: the Big Bad Wolf runs into Granny's house, eats her whole, puts her clothes on and hops into her bed. He tells Little Red Riding Hood to get into bed with him. She thinks her granny looks weird but gets in anyway, and he attacks and eats her whole. Full with his meal of grandmother and granddaughter, the Big Bad Wolf falls asleep. A passing hunter hears the wolf snoring loudly and goes into the house to investigate. He can't find the women, sees the wolf dressed in drag and deduces that he has eaten them. Instead of killing the wolf, he cuts open his belly and releases the women, who are very grateful. He then puts stones in the wolf's stomach and throws him in the river, where he drowns. There is another version that I also like for its gruesomeness: the Big Bad Wolf kills the grandmother, cooks her flesh and blood and hides it in the pantry. When Little Red Riding Hood arrives, the wolf, disguised as the grandmother, invites her to eat this ghastly meal, which she does, not realising what she is eating. This is a little Shakespearean – à la Titus Andronicus. A cat in the house tells her she is disgusting and lets her in on the ruse – she is in fact cannibalising her own grandmother. To make the girl eat Granny suggests that the wolf is quite cross and perverted. Among other things.

There have been various interpretations of the choice of colour for Little Red Riding Hood's cape. Historians have said that in ancient times, children were dressed in red so it was easier to find them. In the seventeenth century, red clothing was the colour of prostitutes, so one theory has her as a child prostitute. Another sees the red cloak as symbolising menstruation, which makes it into a coming-of-age story. Most readings of the story see the red and the wolf as a warning for girls to be careful and vigilant: the red symbolising the blood that is to flow from an attack. The French, as the French often do, prefer the semiotic, or signs and symbols, explanation: recent suggestions opine that the red cloak illuminates the girl's fearless personality and seductive intentions. Actually, in the oldest versions of this story, the cloak wasn't red at all; it was thought that the girl's hair was red, which brings us right back to what men have always known – whatever way you look at it, redheads are trouble.

The red shoes

The colour red is also used to punish girls who have minds of their own. In the medieval story of 'The Red Shoes', Hans Christian Andersen has an orphaned peasant girl adopted by a wealthy old woman. Needless to say, the old lady spoils the girl and the girl grows up with all sorts of flash ideas about herself. She wants to party and dress up and not be stuck with an old woman. She talks her adoptive mother into buying her some outrageous red shoes and proceeds to wear them everywhere; even, rather disrespectfully, to church. However, she goes too far with the red shoes, because instead of looking after her mother when she falls ill and is dying, she goes to a party. But something terrible happens at the party. The red shoes won't stop dancing even when the girl tries to go home. She is forced to dance endlessly – through the streets, out into the countryside – all day and all night. The girl is exhausted with this endless dancing that she can't stop. The red shoes are controlling her – she can't even go to her mother's funeral. Now she really regrets being so vain and headstrong – but, as with all fairytales, things go from bad to worse.

The universe is so furious with her that it sends an angel to tell her that not only is she condemned to dance endlessly for the rest of her life, but the red shoes will continue to force her to dance even after death. By now the girl is desperate and tearing her hair out with the torment, so she dances to an executioner and begs him to chop her feet off. With the feet and red shoes gone, she now has wooden feet and crutches and hobbles off to church to show everyone she has done her penance. But guess what? The severed feet and red shoes continue dancing on their own and prevent her from entering. She tries several Sundays to get into church but is unable to, so decides to work in the priest's house next to the church. That Sunday she stays in her room and prays. She begins hallucinating, believing the church is coming to her room and is happy for the first time since she bought the red shoes. Her heart so fills with divine light, tranquillity and ecstasy that it bursts and at last flies up to heaven where no one cares about her red shoes or her selfish past. This ending is very similar to a famous Edith Piaf song 'Hymne à l'Amour' in which the star-crossed lovers eventually die and go to heaven where there are no more problems and you can love who you want.

'The Red Shoes' ballet version is different again in that it involves a wicked shoemaker but it still centres on a wilful girl who just wants to have fun and not go to church. Most of these fairytales involve religion and are a warning not only to be chaste but also to be God-loving and obedient. The girl sees a fabulous sizzling pair of red shoes in a shop window. She is drawn in and charmed by the shoemaker, who gives them to her as a gift. Thrilled, she puts them on and immediately starts dancing with her boyfriend. They dance off together to a fair, where she dances demonically and unstoppably, not only with her beau but with any other man who will dance with her. She loses sight of the boyfriend, starts hallucinating and can't stop dancing – day and night, through the town, out into the fields. Eventually her clothes become tattered, she is starving and destitute. She dances to a church where a funeral is being held. The priest comes out to help her and she begs him to remove her red shoes. As he removes them, she dies of exhaustion and he carries her into the church (the funeral seems to be for her). The devil shoemaker is there and he takes the shoes back to freshen them up for his next victim.

In 1948 Moira Shearer illuminated the screen in a famous film version of this story – a classic of British cinema. The film is a tale within a tale. A brilliant young ballerina is employed to dance a new ballet called *The Red Shoes*, based on the Hans Christian Andersen fairytale. She herself is conflicted between the man she loves (in other words having a normal happy life) and her professional life, which threatens to be all-consuming. Her ballet master tells her she must choose because dancing is her life and there is no room for human emotion in the repertoire of a truly great dancer. She is passionate about both; her husband and her ballet master are competing for her soul but she feels powerless to choose. Eventually she does choose the ballet and her husband leaves for the train station, devastated. However, at the last moment the ballerina runs out of the ballet in the red shoes to her husband. She rushes into the train station and her husband runs to her, but not fast enough to catch her as she throws herself under a train. As she lies dying, she asks her husband to remove the red shoes. The ballet master, realising what he has done, goes ahead with the show as a mark of respect to her, using a spotlight in the place she would have been dancing.

Surrender Dorothy

And then, let us not forget the most sparkling pair of red shoes ever – Dorothy's ruby slippers in *The Wonderful Wizard of Oz*. Misunderstood, orphan Dorothy runs away from her Kansas home, ends up in a tornado and finds herself whisked up into the magical land of Oz. She meets all sorts of people there including Glinda the Good Witch of the North, who has killed the Wicked Witch of the East and nicked her ruby slippers. She knows these red shoes will eventually help Dorothy in her quest to get back home to Kansas and has them transferred to Dorothy's feet. These shoes have magical powers, needless to say. The Wicked Witch of the West turns up, spitting tacks and claiming the slippers. Dorothy knows that if she takes the ruby slippers off, something terrible will happen. Eventually the time comes when the witch tries to force the shoes off but can't because they appear electrified. She's desperate to get her hands on them and realises she must kill Dorothy to get them and all the power associated with them. Dorothy escapes the witch's clutches and, by the magic of the shoes, is able to return home. Interestingly, in the original book version, the shoes were silver. The famous words 'Surrender Dorothy' were written in the sky by the witch as she rode her broomstick.

In March 2011, on her twenty-fifth birthday, the singer Lady Gaga was given the ruby red shoes Judy Garland wore in the movie. The queen of transformation, Gaga was thrilled because she had wanted to play the role of Dorothy in a school play but the role had gone to someone she considered less deserving. 'When you don't feel like Dorothy today, maybe you feel like someone on the chorus or the Scarecrow or maybe you feel like the Tin Man or the Wicked Witch, just know you will have opportunities in your real life to change things and maybe someone, somebody will hand you a pair of ruby slippers.'

Boudica

The greatest red-haired woman of all was the Celtic warrior queen Boudica, which means victorious. She first went to war against the Romans in about AD 61. She was highly intelligent, imposingly tall, had a voice drenched in caustic soda, an iron-hearted stare and thick, tangled red hair down to her hips. She probably started off being a sweet woman prone to a quick temper when she was married to King Prasutagus of the Iceni people in the area that is now Norfolk. But when he died and the Romans raided and pillaged their territory, flogged Boudica and raped her daughters in public, she became very cross. Her husband had done a deal with the Romans where, rather than be taken over by them, they both came to an agreement that he and his family would continue to run Iceni during his life and after his death. This agreement, however, was not honoured by the Romans, who simply marched in and took the kingdom as if it had been conquered. They treated the people badly, called in dodgy loans, diverted rivers so only they could swim in them and reduced the people to starvation and slavery on their own land.

The fierce Boudica girded herself with her tunic and golden necklace and went forth to haemorrhage her rage on any Roman-controlled part of Britain she could find. She would roar into town in her scythed war chariot with her daughters seated on either side and her rebel troops in behind, asserting her desire to avenge her loss of liberty, her physical abuse and the sexual assault of her daughters. Let me draw a scythed chariot for you: it was a modified war chariot with one-metre-long blades sticking out of the wheels horizontally and sometimes also pointing out from under the driver's seat. When this invention ploughed full-speed through an opposing battle line, the soldiers were cut in half.

Armed thus, Boudica screamed 'victory or death'. First of all she raided Camulodunum, now Colchester, and mercilessly demolished it. Rubbing her blood-drenched hands through her red hair, she moved onto Londinium, now London, and burnt it to the ground, slaughtering anyone in her way. Very cross. Next Boudica set her sights on the town that is now St Albans, Verulamium, and wiped out 80,000 people. Eighty thousand! She didn't believe in taking prisoners and reserved her most gruesome tortures for noble Roman women. They had depraved parties in sacred Roman places where prisoners were impaled on spikes and had their breasts cut off and sewn to their mouths. Cripes. Boudica was eventually defeated and accounts have her either poisoning herself or falling sick and dying. In any case, there was a huge, ostentatious funeral. She was really missed.

The future of red hair

Redheads should be proud of their heritage, in part because it is so unusual. They are uniquely special with their ethereal, timeless beauty. Globalisation forces us towards certain trends in food, architecture and financial systems. Redheads need to stand out and show that they can't be made to conform to the accepted definitions of blonde or brunette beauty; they should go out of their way to keep the colour brilliant and not let it fade into obscurity. The best way to avoid obscurity and keep the recipe vibrant is to mate with another redhead – otherwise the future will be a valley of tears and an endless darkness of uniformly coloured hair. And it's not just about hair colour, because there is always the dye bottle – it's about the translucent skin and the fine features and that warrior queen don't-fuck-with-me set of genes, which Boudica must have been carrying in duplicate!

How I Stopped Strangling my Mother

Motherhood is a career in conformity from which no amount of subterfuge can liberate the soul without violence.

A Life's Work: On becoming a mother
by Rachel Cusk

The first memory I have of my mother is from when I was a toddler. She was dressed up to go to a ball – short dark hair, very pretty, stylish in a satin evening dress with fur stole, evening purse and lipstick. She was tiny with beautiful collarbones, a long neck and high cheekbones. I thought she was a perfect movie star in her ball dress. How could I know I was going to end up trying to kill her with a sledgehammer? And a kitchen knife. And a sword.

Another memory is of her back. She was wearing an apron and walking away from me and my brother. I was lying on the grass saying goodbye to the blue sky, knowing it was the last time I would see it. Occasional desperate gasps were forced out of my little-girl body as I tried to draw in some air. The gasps weren't getting me anywhere, though, and try as I might, I could feel the life draining out of me as panic quickly took over. The pepper tree, out of which I had fallen while playing Jane to my brother's Tarzan, loomed prettily overhead. I had managed to fall on my back clad in a short safari dress and a crown of leaves. Fortunately the knife I held in my mouth dropped out as I fell.

Every Saturday, my brother David and maybe another younger brother and sister and maybe some neighbourhood kids walked half an hour to the local flea-pit to see a movie. Rain or shine. In our sweaty palms we held shillings to pay for the film plus some lollies. We sat as far back in the cinema as possible, the better to roll Jaffas down the wooden floor. I watched the Tarzan movies very closely for costumes, hairdos, love scenes and dialogue. Afterwards we tramped home, organising production, direction, principal roles and storyline as we went. On arrival in the jungle (our suburban backyard) we would don our costumes, pick up our spears and ropes, instruct the younger children to be lions, tigers, anacondas and rhinos, and act out the movie we had just seen. Quiet, strawberry-blond brother David always got to be Tarzan and control-freak me always got to be Jane – any other kid who thought they were better qualified for the role was quickly subjugated to being either an African cannibal or an Arab ne'er-do-well. Obviously there were no love scenes as no skinny neighbourhood brat was going to get anywhere near me. I was waiting for a real Tarzan. The melodramatic situations we played out were much more interesting to us than our daily lives were generally – we didn't get to kill anyone, save anyone or eat raw meat like Tarzan did in the movie.

I liked playing Jane because she wasn't just a passive damsel in distress – she had adventures herself, was beautiful, swam well and could climb anything, which is how I found myself up the pepper tree hiding from a leopard, holding a knife between my teeth. I lay very still under the tree from which I had fallen; Tarzan and the Africans put their spears down and bent over me. Tarzan knew immediately something was very wrong and ran inside yelling for our mother to come quickly. She strolled out from the kitchen, took a look and said, 'It's an act – she's looking for attention as usual. Ignore her and she'll get up.' From my supine position (I fancied I was going slightly blue by now) I watched my mother walk away. In that moment just before death I realised how wrongly she had read the situation and how much she was going to regret it, and how if I didn't die, I could use it in the battle for supremacy between me and her forever. On the face of it, it was the perfect opportunity for her to be rid of me, the most difficult, precocious child in the world. As I started convulsing, Tarzan grabbed me, forced me into a sitting position and thumped me really hard on the back (how did a little kid know to do that?). I gasped and choked; another thump and I spluttered into life. After that episode, I was indeed in a slightly superior tactical position in the Oedipal competition with the mother. But only temporarily. She, needless to say, was mortified that she had got it so wrong but nevertheless reminded me that, strictly speaking, it was my fault as I had cried wolf once too often. After this, she enrolled me in drama classes so I could more readily access my inner Jane.

• • •

If my mother had lipstick and Chanel No. 5 on, then the occasion must have been important. Chanel No. 5: the most famous perfume in the world, the perfume my grandmother wore and the one I still wear. The lipstick was applied for Mass, bringing a new baby home from the hospital and marching down to my primary school to sort out the nuns. As far as my mother was concerned, she alone was responsible for running the parish, greasing up to priests, preventing nuns from getting flash ideas about themselves, keeping my father on what she imagined was a tight leash, and reminding me, her eldest daughter, that I was expected to excel. In absolutely everything. The most common sentence my mother said to me was, 'Is that the best you can do? What is 80 per cent supposed to mean?' My most common sentence (with slouched shoulders) was, 'But I studied so hard, Mum.' That was always a lie. My most common thought regarding my mother was, *Can someone please get this vice grip off me?* Living with Mother was like living in a game show, which could be exciting sometimes but one false move could make you lose thousands.

My mother, a repressed eccentric, ensured we got mixed messages all our childhoods. Every night after we had done the dinner dishes, we all knelt on the dining room floor and said the rosary together because 'The family that prays together, stays together'. How could someone who was artistic and wore beautiful fur stoles and lipstick kneel on the floor? This is why I now have crap knees, as do my five brothers and sisters. That and endless hours on our knees at Mass, begging the Irish passion-killers to release us from impure thoughts, and reflecting on some hapless girl saint who chose to be stabbed thirty-six times rather than be touched by a man. When my osteopath asks about the medical history of my crap knees and neck, I say, 'Ask the Virgin Mary.' Three thousand, four hundred Hail Marys . . . how could any knee survive that? My father was worse. He converted to Catholicism from Church of England (which caused his family to practically have a collective breakdown), then went to Mass *every morning* in his manic phase. Even my mother thought this was above and beyond the call of duty. They have lived together for sixty-three years and even now can't agree on which church to attend Sunday Mass at – he goes to one, she to another. It's a matter of priest preference – who has time to generate such a preference? She can't drive any more, so he goes to Mass, comes home, takes her to Mass, doesn't go in, picks her up after Mass.

• • •

One day many years ago, my mother was visiting from Australia, where she and her consort live. I had to take her to church. I had missed a few Masses (about twenty-five years' worth) and turned up in my Jaguar dressed the way I thought you dressed for Mass. I got the look from the mother.

'Where do you think you're going, dear? It's not a cocktail party.'

'What do you mean, Mum, and why aren't you dressed yet?'

'I am dressed – this is how I'm going.'

'What? Where's your lipstick, hat, gloves, best shoes and freshly pressed outfit?'

'Oh, it hasn't been like that for years.'

When we got to the church it was full of people who thought they were at the beach, the priest was friendly and casual and people touched each other and held hands. Held hands! Needless to say, the horror of the situation made me sit on mine. Bad enough I have to 'share' with the hairdresser and the taxi driver; now the Catholic church, that last bastion of authoritarianism, has gone straight to the dogs, without any help from me at all.

And I haven't even mentioned germs yet – God only knows what would have happened if I had touched all those people. I am a registered nurse. I know how these things work: one minute you're holding some sinner's hand in church and the next you're in a coma in the infectious diseases unit. So I'm sitting on the hard pew in a designer outfit, red lipstick on, with my mother sitting next to me, in slacks, sandals and a blouse. I'm hoping that hospitals are open on Sunday and imagining the conversation with the emergency doctor:

'Have you been in the tropics lately, Ms Mathias?'

'No. I got this tapeworm from kissing a Catholic, doctor. My mother said it would be safe, but she's lied before.'

Anyway, I'm wondering what God must be thinking about this display of casual attitudes and slovenly postures, when suddenly there's an outbreak of what could only be described as jubilant singing. It was only half a centimetre away from talking in tongues. In my day you sang dirges designed to remind you of the fate that awaits us all – no clapping, no smiling and no moving, thank you very much. To this day I still love mournful laments – they make me feel happy – and I will still go into a cathedral anywhere in the world if I am passing by and there is a good choir singing. I whispered to my mother, 'Someone's going to get cured of leprosy any minute – I can feel it. And with all this hand-holding going on, you better not be the last one they touched.'

'Why do you have to exaggerate everything?'

'You made me like this.'

'Don't start.'

'Do you remember those huge boils I got from school when I was seven? They practically had aliens crawling out of them. I bet I got them in church from some low-life pimply kid whose mother kept her babies in cardboard boxes.'

'What boils? Everybody got boils in those days.'

In those days is why half the country is now covered in scars. Boil scars. I can still feel the heat and smell the clay of the poultices and the freshly laundered bandages. Those boils could have gone into my spinal cord and my brain resulting in endocarditis and pneumonia with a blood-curdling death swiftly following. Okay, so it was only a boil but a child doesn't know they are looking death in the face.

One of my sisters is much worse with germs than I am. Take the incident with the cloves. We're cooking Christmas dinner and I'm helping with the ham. My sister has taken the ham from the spotlessly clean fridge and cooked it for three hours in a flour and water crust in the perfectly clean oven. We've removed the skin (I'm surprised she let me keep my rings on for this), scored the fat and it's time to stick the cloves in. I take the packet and dump some cloves on the spotlessly clean bench. We stick them in the ham and there are about a dozen left over so I start putting them back in the packet.

'You're not putting those back in the packet are you, Pete?'

'Yeah. Why?'

'Throw them away.'

'Why?'

'They've been on the bench.'

'And?'

'The bench is dirty and now the ones inside the packet are different from the ones outside.'

'The bench is perfectly clean.'

'Not really – not if you look closely.'

• • •

My sisters and brothers, as far as I was concerned, were strangers placed in my home to get in my way, as were my parents. I told everyone I was an only child. Every time the mother brought a new baby home from the hospital I said, 'Mum, is this the last one?'

'Why?' she would ask.

'Because there are far too many children here already.'

'Oh really. Who would you like me to get rid of?'

'You know I can't answer that.'

Privately the answer to that question was, of course, all of them. When we all grew up I discovered my five brothers and sisters were interesting, funny, nice people, none of whom looked like me and none of whom followed remotely connected career paths. They had their kids baptised to cover all bases and have the same relaxed attitude to Catholicism everyone has now. They think it's odd that I can't adjust, that I can't get my teeth off the neck of organised religion, that I feel so rabid about it. Look, I say, I've been to hell and back many times, Catholicism turned me into a control freak with theatrical psychosocial tendencies and an exaggerated sense of occasion, not to mention dress. I'm getting swollen lymph nodes just thinking about it. DON'T TELL ME TO FUCKING RELAX.

• • •

Part of my mother's plan for perfection and excelling-in-everything for me was drama classes – as if living with her, chatting in Latin, fasting, fainting in church and getting a hold on the Holy Trinity concept wasn't dramatic enough. I was enrolled for elocution lessons and joined a theatre group in which I felt perfectly comfortable pretending I was someone else, which of course I was. Anyone else. The elocution lessons were to get rid of my parochial New Zealand accent and help me project my voice, as if I needed any help. I came out of the womb projecting and have been projecting ever since, only now it's with rounded vowels. My mother had perfect enunciation and melodic tone thanks to her elocution lessons. Her parents and eight brothers and sisters in Sydney were amazed by her flash new accent. To this day, I don't speak like any of my brothers and sisters.

In Christian Doctrine lessons at school we explored the intricacies of the Holy Trinity. I was the only one in the class who actually did well in this esoteric subject, having no trouble whatsoever in grasping the concept of a triple personality. I'd been leading a double life since I was five and was fascinated by the idea of pulling off a triple one. I was mesmerised by the Church and its dramatic ostentation – it suited me perfectly. In the drive for perfection, it soon became obvious that I could achieve in narrow areas where I actually had talent, but that I was devoid of ambition. I admired it in other people, but was unable to relate to it personally. My sister now says I always had the killer instinct, but I was certainly unaware of it.

• • •

I chose nursing as my first career mostly because you had to leave home to do it and I thought it was time to start my new life as an only child. What I got terribly wrong was that the nurses' home was crawling with domineering women just like my mother and the nuns, but they disguised themselves in white starch and winged hats – the home sisters. Within the year, the nurses' home got too small and the home sisters got too big, so I decided to go flatting. You would have thought I had announced a wish to hang upside down in hell or tear strips off newborn babies. The matron acted like I was a crime wave just waiting to sweep through and the mother took it as a personal insult. I persisted and moved into a dream flat above a bakery with another nurse. The dining room had rustic-looking curtains and an oak table with flaps; the living room had red check curtains and old armchairs; the twin beds in the bedroom had orange candlewick bedspreads. We were in ecstasy: we were playing house, we were grown-ups, we cooked and entertained and did housework. This was true happiness for a hardened sinner such as myself. At the hospital, I was a hero to the younger nurses because I wore a red petticoat under the wall of white starch – behaviour considered by the matron to be just one slippery step away from Communism. It was my nursing buddies who taught me that men are like linoleum – if you lay them right you can walk over them for the rest of your life. I invited my parents to the flat, cooked a meal and smoothed everything over.

• • •

I'm not sure when the nightmares started – probably in my late teens when I psychologically started to separate myself from childhood. At about the same time I had a religious catharsis and realised I wasn't a Catholic any more. Worse, I didn't believe in God. I hadn't read anything sacrilegious, hadn't been influenced by anyone; it just happened in row six of St Patrick's Cathedral on a Sunday evening at Mass. I had truly believed everything I was told up to that point, then a minute later didn't believe any of it. It was like suddenly having an unprovoked orgasm in church and trying to act like nothing was happening. As I sat there reciting things in Latin I felt exactly like you do after an orgasm – calm, light, relieved and at peace with the world. I floated straight out of there and committed a sin as soon as the opportunity arose, secure in the knowledge that my soul was not destined for hell, meat would no longer stick in my throat on Friday and I was now free to sleep in on Sunday morning. Not only was I not going to hell, I finally understood *there was no hell*. I didn't dare tell my Irish aunts, who I adored – they seemed so attached to hellfire and damnation.

My first true sin of apostasy, or renunciation of one's religion, had already happened. I had to look around for some new ones. I covered envy and gluttony in one day and got sloth and anger under my belt within a week. It was so fantastic to be a jerk, sinful, admit it and not go to hell. Okay, so compared with serious sins like murder and grand larceny I was an underachiever, but lust was about to rear its head. As the years went by, I missed Confession, but soon replaced it with therapists. As I had never committed any great sins before, I knew the priests must have been bored stiff by my tedious confessions of petty lying, embezzlement of piggy banks, disrespect for my betters and impure thoughts. I feel sorry for those priests now, because thanks to my mother training me to be perfect in everything I attempted, I went from being sanctimonious to insubordinate – with exactly the same fervor. If they got hold of some of my imaginary sins now, they wouldn't be falling asleep so fast (Catholics spend their whole lives thinking up outrageous sins so the priest won't have wasted his time). They'd wish the sailors and whores from the nearby docks would come back. I didn't mention my apostasy catharsis to the mother.

• • •

But what to do with a mother? You can't have a catharsis and realise you don't have a mother any more, because your mother is still there, so the purging has to go underground to the deep recesses of the unconscious, there to be processed in dreams. The dreams were extremely violent, psychedelic and loud – suitable for a chainsaw massacre movie. My mother and I would be screaming and hacking at each other with knives, swords and our bare hands. It went on and on and nobody ever won or died – I woke up exhausted and sweating. Possibly the nightmares were so dramatic and colourful because of all the saints' lives and fairytales I had read in which tearing people apart, from limb to limb, was so routine you almost yawned. Possibly they were colourful from all the acid I was dropping. This went on for years until someone finally pointed out to me that I needed to be a bit more proactive. It was suggested I go into therapy and stop stamping my feet.

In therapy I got it all out and threw five-year-old-type tantrums and killed and buried the mother. After that, the dreams stopped and never came back again. That's why I believe in therapy and highly recommend burying anyone who annoys you. Jumping on the grave is also helpful. When middle-aged women tell me they still have problems with their mothers I am astounded. They should both go into therapy, spit it out and grow up. Conflict with your mother when you're over thirty-five is the both of you stuck in a childhood relationship of the past. Your brain has moved on but your emotions haven't. Blaming your mother keeps you passive and dependent and unable to take responsibility for your own life. Parent-baiting is a waste of energy and prevents you from taking a look at the bad choices you made in life of your own free will. Parents, especially mothers, can only do their best and psychologists say that 'good enough' is good enough in most cases. In order to forgive the mother and release her from your outrageously high expectations, the daughter must go back and try to remember what was going on in the mother's life at that time – maybe the family was broke, maybe the father was a philanderer, maybe the mother was sick, maybe you the daughter were so bloody temperamental that no mother would have got on with you, no matter how saintly she was. You also have to take into consideration what your mother's mother was like. I am the most immature person in the universe, so if I can stop blaming my mother, anyone can. However, if your mother refuses to grow up then give up and back off, maybe forever – life is too short to put up with recidivist matriarchs.

What made it easier in the end is that my mother, to her great credit, also changed and met me halfway. She put up with my nastiness and arrogance and became very tolerant about my sinning. We slowly got to a stage where we could actually make jokes about the past; she apologised for her excesses and I for mine. Now she makes me sign my books to her: 'To my beloved mother, who was always so good to me' – then falls about with laughter. An apology from a mother, even a half-hearted one, goes a long way. I have trained her so well that she seems to have gone back to the person she possibly was before motherhood changed her. Before marriage, that is pre-1948, my mother made her own ball gowns by laying fabric on the floor and cutting it out, had a blonde streak in her dark hair, tattooed a blue beauty spot on her cheek, and painted butterflies on her fingernails. Her daughters have inherited her love of sewing, crafting and maintaining a beautiful home. Post children, that is from the 1980s onward, she started painting very well, telling risqué jokes, which sometimes have the word 'fuck' in them, and now at ninety-two goes line dancing even though macular degeneration ensures she can see practically nothing. The problem was the intervening years of exhausting motherhood.

In a way, mothers breed daughters to be their alter ego – they subconsciously produce someone to succeed where they failed. My mother, who was prevented from realising her artistic dreams by her father, bent over backwards to give me an artistic education – drama, singing, elocution, music, French, dancing – then got rather cross when I turned out to be a dramatic, articulate, musical and head-strong young lass. Simone de Beauvoir said that the double (the daughter) is a 'dubious replacement who assassinates' the original (the mother). Sometimes, I think my mother – the mother I knew as a child – is a figment of my imagination. She was popular with my friends – I couldn't believe how different she was with them. With the exception of a few dissidents, when most of my friends meet my mother they say everything I have told them about her is a lie, that she is just a sweet little old lady. She couldn't possibly have been as difficult as I have described. To this day, when older people who knew my mother when we were children describe her they call her interesting, intelligent, lively and beautiful. The mother is a woman's first and most powerful role model; there is no getting around it, whether you both like it or not. The mother–daughter business is never ever over – it ain't over till the fat lady sings and the fat lady sings at the funeral. Every time I write a new book, I send the first copy to my parents as if to say, 'See?' My father asks, 'What page is the sex on?' and my mother says, 'There's a mistake on page seventy-three.'

• • •

Some people consider dreams to be symbolic and hardly ever literal, so when you dream of someone else, it is not necessarily them, it is a part of you symbolised by that person. A person who is killing the mother is seeking release from their own hang-ups in a double-edged way, because it is both revenge and self-liberation. In a way you *have* to kill the mother to grow up. Dreaming of death signifies the ending of one phase so that another can begin. Dreaming of killing the mother can also represent the 'death' of the motherly side of your own nature. According to some dream analysis, the weapons of attack used in my dreams are indicative. The sword signifies authority, protection and power, but also the spirit and a need to get rid of some aspect of your life. Strangling relates to not being able to express yourself and being strangled means you are being denied fulfilment. Stabbing symbolises deep anger and aggression. The violence of the dream fight suggests unexpressed rage, but the interesting thing was in my dreams my mother was always attacking as viciously as I was – she wasn't passively taking the bash, she was enthusiastically participating in the bash. I wonder what dreams she was having at this period? She was probably asking herself how long she would be sent down for if she actually strangled me.

Most psychologists say dream symbolism is rubbish – dreams are simply your mind processing the events of the day or sometimes the past. Dreaming happens during the REM (rapid eye movement) phase of sleep – the muscles are paralysed and the brain activity increases. Dreams are mixed up and often don't make sense, which could be related to the synapses being all mixed up during REM. All very well, but the problem with my nightmares was that they were resolving nothing and I wasn't moving on to the next phase – whatever that was. It took a trained therapist to bash it all on the head. It not only released me from the nightmares but improved my relationship with my real mother and helped shrivel the guilt. The reason it worked was because it wasn't a dream – it was real life and a chair took the place of the mother. When I was a therapist at a drug and alcohol treatment centre in Canada, I had to go into therapy as part of my training. This was encounter therapy, fashionable in those days along with frizzy perms, being at one with the universe and eating alfalfa sprouts.

'All right,' smiled the therapist. We were all sitting on hard chairs in a circle in the therapy room. 'You seem to be an angry person, Peta. Who are you angry at?'

'Angry? No I'm not. Maybe. I can't choose. There are too many people and we could be here till September.'

'We have all day and the next day if you wish.'

'I don't want to do this. I'm staff here and I don't want to talk about this stuff in front of other people. In fact, I don't want to talk about it at all. I'm afraid of opening the floodgates.'

'You're safe here. No one will judge you. If you express the anger, it will no longer control your life.'

You wish, I thought. Birds outside were chirping and the group of about ten people sat quietly staring at me, waiting for the filth to pour out. 'You're not going to make me cry. Okay, so I'm a little bit angry, but I'm over it. I can handle it.'

Staring at me: 'Why are your legs crossed and your arms folded? Let it out.'

Under this slow pressure, gentle reader, I chose a sort of collage of persons I was angry at, including my mother, the grocer and every nun I had ever met, but I couldn't get myself worked up about it. The therapist then put a chair in the middle of the circle and told me to choose a particular person and I could say anything I liked to them. I could say everything awful I had never said but desperately wanted to say. No one else in the room knew the person and no one cared.

Half an hour later I snapped back into the present to find myself on the floor with everyone's hands resting gently on me. I was soaked in tears and sweat, my hair was in a huge bird's nest and my body felt like it had been in a fist fight. The chair was broken in a corner of the room and I was possessed by a desperate thirst.

'What happened?' I croaked. 'Is everyone still alive?'

'Everyone's fine. Everyone's alive and well. How do you feel?' asked the therapist.

'Great. Tired. Hungry.'

They sat on the floor silently watching me.

'You went back to your childhood and you really had it in for a few people.'

I have to say it was a very powerful tool and amazing to spew all that stuff out for the first time. It was fabulous to throw a major tantrum and not get punished. My dealing to these people from my childhood gave me a clue to something mysterious in my heart, but I kept that to myself. I had had a confrontation with my anima and got in touch with a few demons, but I hadn't said it all, I hadn't revealed it all. There was a lot more pus to be extracted but time would probably deal with that. I wanted to clean the sludge out but didn't know if I could face the invasion of a psychiatrist. As it turns out, if you've got the emotional intelligence God gave gravel, it only takes a small intervention to make a major change. Killing people in dreams is a waste of time really. It has to be done in waking life, which doesn't necessarily mean you have to confront the person concerned – replacements work just as well, strangely enough. If you *really* kill your mother you will be subjected to a life of bad food, small spaces and dodgy tattoos.

● ● ●

My conflict with my mother is not original or different – most mothers and daughters have tugs-of-war and it starts right from birth. The first snaps of anger appear as young as eight months and are an ordinary part of development. How could you not have conflict? Mother has produced inside her body a copy of herself. She knows what she went through to get to womanhood and she wants to protect you from harm and hurt. The daughter doesn't want to be protected – ideally she wants to be treated like her brothers, who are not over-protected. Some daughters have naturally calm, easy-going temperaments and are happy to be compliant. If you are not one of those girls, you experience the restrictions, the instructions on how to behave, how to dress, how to think in a lady-like way, as intolerable. Unless the girl is genetically very sweet-natured, she will react to her mother's controlling behaviour with anger. We've all heard the stories of little girls (hardly ever boys) saying to their mothers, 'You can't be my mother. I was adopted.' This is the girl furious that she cannot control her mother so she's looking for another, easier one. I used to actually pack a knapsack when I ran away from home. It was such a routine occurrence that in the end my mother would help me pack the bag, making sure I had lots of nuts and raisins. Sometimes I would leave home for a tree, sometimes a friend and sometimes the bush. Eventually, I had to go home, because I didn't know how to do my hair.

I don't think I've improved much, but my mother has gone from being someone I never wanted to be like to someone I admire and hope I end up like. The older I get the more of her I recognise in myself, and that no longer terrifies me. I have absolutely inherited her toughness and forthrightness and snappy impatience. I hope I have inherited her looks too, because at ninety-two she has an almost unlined face and perfect posture. She is so determined to remain fit that she walks around and around the house and garden for half an hour every day, because she can't walk down the road any more thanks to blindness. I imagine I shall finish my days walking to the wine shop and back for exercise, or doing swimming-pool exercises in the old people's home with a gin bottle strapped to my leg. We both said the truth to each other and let go the need for the other to be perfect and not disappointing, and neither of us died in the process.

I was very conservative in my expectations of my parents. When my youngest sister addressed my parents as 'Ann' and 'Harvey' as a teenager, I just stared at her with my mouth open. When my father asked her what time she would be home from a party and she replied, 'I'll be home when I'm home, Harvey', with a sweet smile, I shrieked at my mother, 'If I had said that to you as a teenager, I would have been burned alive!'

I'm shocked my mother even reads my books, what with their graphic sex passages and her cameo appearances. In fact, when I call my parents in Sydney to announce my latest book, I say to my mother, 'Mum, don't read the chapter on sex. You won't understand it.' They call back a week later, having gone straight to the sex chapter, and say, 'You are so right dear – I didn't understand a thing. I can't imagine how we made six children without your advice.'

My mother is strong, both physically and mentally; she's positive, accepting of life's vicissitudes with grace and courage. Actually, she is bionic – to mention the phoenix would not be gilding the lily. She breaks shoulders, falls over, has hip replacements, benign cancers, gets very sick and pale, recovers, is razor-sharp mentally, loses money, gets money, still tells me how she would prefer my hair to be, still comments on the literacy of my writing. She's the size of a toothpick and very fragile, but still enjoying the services of her man slave, my father, who is still fond of saying, 'I don't ask questions; I just obey.'

Letter to my Much Younger Self

I wish I wish I wish in vain
I wish I were a maid again
But a maid again I shall never be
Until apples grow on an ivy tree.

'Love is Teasing' (traditional Irish song)

Dear Peta,

At the age of twenty-five you flee Auckland for Vancouver to escape phlegmatic New Zealand, a philandering man and a destiny of marriage, children, murder, mayhem and gin. You run with open arms to a place not so different from Auckland, but anywhere, you think, is better than an island at the bottom of the Earth. This trip doesn't clear your head, though: you fill in the forms, answer the questions and emigrate. It's a good idea to remove yourself from the man, but you don't go far enough. You later realise you should have gone to the moon.

Vancouver turns out to be a bigger Auckland, so in the quest to get closer to the moon, you move to Montreal. As soon as you get off the plane you see that the people in Montreal are different – they are olive-skinned and dark-haired, or golden-skinned and fair-haired, and these people speak Italian, Portuguese, Chinese, Lebanese, French and Hungarian. The pace is faster, more nervous, noisier. This is more like it. This is what you have in mind in your quest for adventure, excitement and romance. You want a sea change and Montreal provides instant colour, stimulation and camouflage.

You love all these foreign people instantly, and far from feeling dépaysée, you feel much less like a foreigner and misfit than you do in New Zealand. For once you are the least different-looking of everyone, and Montrealers not only look different, they dress different. They are fashionable and chic, making you take a second look at your antipodean, hippy, braless, long-tressed look. The men prove to be *very* different. The Italians call out to you in the street, whistle, toot and stare. Being a staunch hippy feminist, you are horrified and yell 'Sexist, chauvinist, Roman pig-dogs' while giving them the international finger signal. They are enchanted. You could have slightly eased up on that because when you hit fifty, you start whistling back, grateful for the attention.

The English Protestant Montrealers are similar to New Zealanders, but that is only a visual trick because they don't understand you when you speak. Having a great sense of humour, Montrealers fall over themselves to make fun not only of your incomprehensible New Zealand vowels but also your general naïveté. 'Say "sex",' they scream. 'Sucks,' you say. 'Say "dance",' they scream. 'Dahnce,' you say. 'Say "fish",' they scream. 'Fush,' you say. Half of Quebec is French Catholic, but in Montreal when you arrive they all speak English and French. Whereas ten years later they will speak primarily French. You will be grateful for this. Within ten years you will speak fluent French and be married to a Frenchman.

You love the city's wide leafy streets, extreme muggy-hot and freezing-cold climate, terraced houses with steps up the front, and the open, friendly people. You don't drive so take the bus everywhere, thus experiencing the city at much closer range than most people would ever want to. Montreal is full of chic boutiques, sidewalk cafés with menus in foreign languages, endless discos, bars, great dress shops, international restaurants and beautiful old buildings. You visit art galleries, buy French clothes from the sublime shops on Saint Catherine Street and go to McGarrigle sisters folk concerts with your new friends. You enjoy Arctic cold and central heating and stifling heat and air conditioning for the first time in your life. You go into the underground Métro to keep warm.

You stay for a while with Jane and Dave who live on Rue Saint Laurent in Old Montreal. Dave is a gentle, tender giant who writes poems to Jane and once lined her walls with tin foil because she wanted a little more light. He always dresses in black, is in advertising, hates it and is brilliant at it. Jane is a small, colourful, slightly nutty woman who dresses in tie-dyed clothes and has frizzy hair. She is the only other person you know who gets angrier than you when men get on her nerves. In the past she had deliberately driven a car into a tree that her lover was standing next to, had tried to burn another's house down and pulled most of the hair out of a rival's head. Dave and Jane live in a rather grand apartment with wide corridors, lots of light and large white rooms. Jane called their first child Pagan but Dave put his foot down when she wanted to call the second one Christian. The kids are as sharp as razors and talk non-stop in French, telling dirty jokes that their nanny teaches them. You don't understand but laugh generously out of love. This is the first time you have ever lived in a home without a backyard and lemon trees. In fact, it is the first time you have ever paid for a lemon. Pagan and her brother make up for the lack of outdoors by throwing themselves up and down the stairs and chucking pot plants at each other. The nanny teaches you how to cook a steak the French way, which necessitates heating butter in an iron frying-pan till you can't see the kitchen any more.

'Bon, is perfect. Now, Peta, you can put 'er in. Ze steak. Put 'er in.'

You follow her voice and throw the steaks in from a safe distance, then run out.

'Where you go? You 'ave to turn 'er over . . . Viens là, viens.'

'But Lucette, I put them in,' you splutter, waving smoke out of your eyes. '*You* take them out.'

The kids scream with delight at the cooking lesson. You have tears streaming down your face and the steaks are black on the outside and red everywhere else. With pride, Lucette removes the steaks from the pan, pours the black butter over them and serves them up. You think surely it is time to call for Chinese takeaways.

Your money lasts a few months; then you find a job. All you are qualified for is nursing, but you are loath to sink to that level unless an emergency presents itself. One night at a bar (you are wearing an op-shop dress and chopsticks in your long black hair), you meet a woman who is a counsellor. This woman is as mad as a snake and couldn't have helped an amoeba so (as is totally standard in these professions) she has a senior position in a youth counselling agency. When you look at the mess she called a life it is obvious you could do a better job with your eyes sewn together. As you are still suffering from your missionary complex, you take her advice and apply for a position as Child Care Counsellor at a drop-in centre funded by local government, called 'The House'. The position requires someone with a medical background because the youths keep slitting their necks shaving and causing all sorts of damage such as pregnancies, bad breath and mistaken identity due to excessive pimples. Having never applied for a job in your life, you discover you have quite a flair for the interview game. Basically, the person who has the most confidence, in spite of the fact that they may have the least qualifications, is the person who gets the job. Twenty years later, research shows that this is absolutely true. Also, even though you are a fully paid-up feminist, you see no reason why you should not smile nicely, slap a bit of lipstick on and throw in a few womanly wiles. As it turns out in subsequent years, this interview technique rarely fails. You take great pleasure in manipulating the game so that you are doing the interviewing.

This is how you will enter the world of fourteen-year-old alcoholics, child-mothers and curing by camping. You can barely stand normal children, so aren't sure how to cope with disturbed ones. You have to teach the boys to spell well enough to do graffiti, after coming into your office one day to find I HATE GRILS spray-canned all over the walls. *Oh for God's sake*, you think, *what a bunch of losers*. You go on camping trips to the KOA camping ground where the staff get up to more tricks than the hooligans, the tent ropes get eaten through by beavers and foxes, and Quebec almost burns down as a result of creative camp-fire techniques. But hey! At least God's misunderstood children are getting personality tips and not trying to have sex with anything that moves, which leads to you deciding to initiate sex education classes. These are met with mild hysteria and result in an increase in your sexual vocabulary by 80 per cent. You call the classes 'relationship management', which is rather ambitious as no adult has ever suggested the concept of responsibility or choice to these delinquents. They gasp when you tell them about the clitoris and that women can basically have orgasms indefinitely, the only thing stopping them being tiredness. Men, on the other hand, are to be pitied as they can only have one or two then die. At this information they all lie down on the floor and scream.

At the same time that you start the counselling job at The House, you leave Jane and Dave's place and move into a communal dwelling on Rue Saint François Xavier. You find this apartment on the bulletin board of the nearby health food shop. The announcement reads: WANTED. WOMAN TO JOIN THREE WILD, FEMINIST, HEDONISTIC, GORGEOUS WOMEN IN BEAUTIFUL TWO-STOREYED APARTMENT. How do they know you are there? Bonny, Beth, Shelley and you take one look at each other and fall instantly in love. The apartment has a kitchen, dining room, lounge, bathroom, two bedrooms downstairs and two bedrooms up. It is an old, funky brick building full of comfy furniture and books. You have rarely lived with women only and wonder why. It is so easy. In a household of all women the housework always gets done, the food is great, the toilet seat is always down and there are never any scenes. Bonny, who is a filmmaker and artist, has the real Jewish look of olive skin, dark curly hair, almond eyes and generous mouth. Beth, the actress, is not beautiful but has that thing that tall, dramatic women have: carriage and great vowels, like Vanessa Redgrave. Shelley, with the long dark hair and cat-like eyes, has been around and is a late student of medicine. Bonny will sharpen up your feminist principles; Beth has been to France as an exchange student and introduces you to buttery croissants and brioche; and Shelley will change forever your teeth-cleaning habits. Her bedroom is next to the bathroom and it is devilishly hard to concentrate on scrubbing while she is loudly making love next door.

Nearby where you live is a lovely little park, the centre of civilisation for the neighbourhood. And of course, as with everywhere in Montreal, most of the neighbours are Portuguese and Eastern Europeans, thrown in with artists, writers and musicians all living in gaudy houses. At the end of the block is a plant shop, two second-hand clothing shops, a leather shop, a weaving shop and a quilt shop. Also, there are two Chinese, one Greek, one Italian, one Lebanese and one Polish restaurant. It is here you will learn to eat borscht, blinis, pierogi and bigos. In the street the kids play and bash each other up with big pieces of wood called hockey sticks. McGill University area nearby is teeming with colourful students, the proletariat and immigrants. Restaurants, pastry shops and delicatessens, the best of which is Schwartzes on Saint Laurent Street (which makes the most succulent smoked-meat sandwiches in the world), line the streets. You go in at two in the morning for a sandwich and people are there in ball gowns. The cheap stores on Saint Laurent are palaces of delight for the flamboyant such as you, overflowing with peasant scarves, coloured pantyhose, tin bowls with flowers on them, lace curtains and ethnic rugs for your floors.

You and the new flatmates enjoy each other's company so much that men feel they are almost intruding when they come visiting. You lie in the sun on the roof reading passages from *The Second Sex* and *Fear of Flying* to each other and discuss your relationships in graphic detail. Bonny of the huge smile and raven curls is seeing the boy across the road who is a doctor. Beth has two boyfriends and is rather earnest and dramatic but not beyond a little flippancy. Shelley has various boyfriends, one of whom she dumps because she doesn't like the way he turns his jeans up. Leonard Cohen lives down the road. You have the best parties in the neighbourhood, cook the best food and are intoxicated with the power of being young, free and loving your lives. It is 1975 and you are twenty-five. For your part, ambivalence will be the order of the day in your half-hearted attempts to communicate with the opposite sex. Your flight from the philandering man in New Zealand is too recent and you haven't entirely left him in your heart or head. You should have cut him out of your heart with an oyster knife and had a lobotomy, because you will continue torturing each other for many years. Your relationship will become so famous for its toxicity that your friends change his name to The-Man-Who-Ruined-Peta's-Life, and introduce him as such at parties.

One sweltering Montreal day you will wander into a very

special, magical shop. It is called Salmagundy and true to its name sells a mixture of antiques, clothes and eclectic giftware. There are bird cages with live birds in them, brass bedsteads, antique books, lamp shades covered with Sanderson fabric, unusual toys, expensive writing paper. Entranced and seduced, you spend half an hour wandering around before a voice says, 'Hello would you like a glass of wine?' Seated behind the counter, a woman beams up at you and hands you a crystal glass of wine on a silver platter and from then on in you are inseparable. Lynne is a serious hedonist and lives for the sensual experience – books, restaurants, travel, theatre, art, beauty. She is very little with a dark bob and heart-shaped face. She's given to extravagant gestures and storytelling.

You eat at Greek restaurants opened by expatriates. These restaurants are by and large cheap but some of them are very chic, up-market and serve beautiful food rarely seen in Greece, you later find out. Gorgeous, sophisticated dark-haired men play backgammon at the bar and at low tables, smoking diminutive Greek cigarettes and drinking endless tiny cups of thick, sweet coffee. Greek men and women are warm and charming in an openly fervent way that to a girl like you, brought up in an emotional vice grip, seems almost perverted. You are hopeless at card games and gambling, because you aren't competitive and don't care whether you win or lose. But you do have a flair for backgammon, playing with your new Greek friends all night, sipping gloopy ouzo and learning how to be passionate about a tiny thing with dots on it. You and your friends also do breakfast crawls in the winter on Sunday mornings during which you eat different courses in different restaurants, interspersed with walks in Mount Royal Park and classical concerts at Marie-Reine-du-Monde Cathedral. It takes all day. You weep into your Jewish poppyseed cake, so happy are you in your new home, Montreal.

It is during one of these all-day breakfasts that you and your friends take it into your heads to drive out of town for a little holiday to Lynne and George's farm. By now you are firm friends with Lynne from Salmagundy. Husband George is a lot younger and the opposite of her in every way. Where she is tiny he is huge; where she is extrovert he is reserved; where she couldn't cook a carrot he is a real epicurean with quite the dainty palate. He is quiet but loves practical jokes, which she finds unsophisticated and embarrassing. She lives her busy social and business life in Montreal during the week and every Friday drives an hour and a half to Shawbridge to spend the weekend in the countryside where he lives his quiet domestic life, selling plants and seedlings from the farm. Upon arrival in the late afternoon you find drinks and warm, tantalising country cooking waiting for you. George is a born homemaker and between them he and Lynne have created a farmhouse that is a haven of good taste and graciousness. You die for your invitations there, diving immediately into the kitchen with George upon arrival.

After replenishing yourself on the likes of roast duck and macadamia pie, you rest yourself on plump feather beds with antique paisley quilts.

Fascinated by your new culture and wishing to immerse yourself totally like any good new arrival, not to mention being a naïve New Zealand girl, you believe everything you are told. On this visit George offers to take you skite hunting and really it is unforgivable that no one has thought to take you before. A skite hunt is an important part of Canadian cultural assimilation. It is more of an ambush than a search, necessitating vigilant undercover trap-setting as the skite is an elusive, cunning little creature. Just how elusive you soon find out. If this is a rite of passage, then you have to do it. The hunt has to happen at night as the animal is nocturnal and the equipment involves a large potato sack, a torch, gumboots and a very warm overcoat. You are also permitted to take biscuits to eat as it sometimes takes a long time to catch a skite. None of this information will seem suspect to you, so you jump in George's car on a freezing Quebecois night and drive to the forest outside Shawbridge for your exciting adventure. You later find out Lynne was so concerned about your safety out alone in the freezing forest that she nearly spilt the beans. At no point do you think to ask why you are catching a skite and what you are supposed to do with it, once caught.

In the half-hour drive to the forest, wrapped up to resemble a bear hunter going to Outer Mongolia, George outlines his foul play to you. He explains in detail how you have to go into the darkest part of the forest with the torch, sit down with the potato sack open between your legs, turn the torch off and wait. As soon as the skite runs into the sack you are to quickly tie it up and whistle for him to come and get you. Success is the difference between being an intrepid Canadian stalwart and a spoilt New Zealand pussy, no good to anything but a few sheep. He waits at the edge of the forest as too many people around frighten the animal. In order to attract the skite, George shows you how to beat the earth and bushes with a big stick while making a sucking noise with your mouth. *Still* you do not click. Dear Peta, you will sit there in the wet dark forest, alone, rigid with fear, a lamb to the slaughter of his trickery. He, meanwhile, goes back to the car, paralytic with the humour of it, to drink beer and wipe the tears from his face. After about twenty minutes he can bear it no longer and goes in to save you. He tries to admonish you for being a failure and a useless hunter, but falls over in the bush into a heap of prolonged laughter. This episode, which will send Lynne and George into paroxysms every time they think of it, is another lesson to you. You are shocked at your inability to see the trap even though it is only a game. In terms of strategy it is simple; it just involves trust, love and a simple lure. The lure of acceptance. It is powerlessness in the nicest possible way, but still you have been had. You laugh, though, because one doesn't wish to be seen as a bad sport. You shouldn't have worried about your naïveté, because it won't last long.

Another time Lynne and you decide to just get on a plane and visit friends in California. San Francisco is exploding with colour, the inhabitants are loose and spilling out onto the footpaths from coffee shops and corner bars and the Victorian houses are slashes of yellow, brown, pink, blue and black. Every corner you turn there are fabulous shops, pottery, foreign food, street music, flower power and little neighbourhood hangouts. Reggae music has just hit America and you will dance all night in your flowing dresses to its intoxicating gunga rhythm. The West Coast of America is spearheading the fledgling therapy industry. Everyone is touchy-feely and into 'getting in touch with their feelings', which will be new stuff to you but you think *What the hell, go with the flow man and get in touch*. It turns out to be a repulsive experience and almost turns Lynne off you for life.

You look up your friend Philip from whose childhood parties in Auckland you had been banned for inciting riotous behaviour and free-economy thinking. There he is, living in San Francisco thinking he is the greatest thing since sliced bread, making you eat pavlova – that glutinous mass of pure sugar held together with a few egg whites. There he is with his actor friends forcing overcooked New Zealand roast lamb into your person. For old time's sake you insist on having peas and potatoes with the roast and ask if they have any frozen peas in the freezer.

'Are you kidding? The only thing we have in this freezer is dope, coffee and film canisters.' Silly you. He grabs you and hugs you very tight the way New Zealanders do. 'Peta, darling, it's so wonderful to see you. You're so grown up and shapely now. The last time we were in the same room together . . .'

'Yeah, yeah I know, I was being thrown out of it.'

'But that was only after you opened my parents' gate and told all the little children at my birthday party to go and find you some money from the neighbours.'

'I needed the money to buy props for the play I was putting on. A girl has to do what's necessary in terms of fundraising. And what about you, you pathetic suck? I seem to remember major tittle-tattling on your part.'

'That's not true. I never. I admired you.'

You stupid girl. It makes me weep to think of all the years you will waste being a nurse and a counsellor and a cook in the hot hard kitchens of the world. Your missionary complex will unfortunately stall your using the abilities you were born with – entertaining and drama making. It isn't till you are forty-five that you finally become who you were supposed to be – a writer and television presenter. At eight years old you were directing, producing, acting, singing in your own productions, not to mention designing wardrobe and negotiating funding. Talk about arrested development.

Philip visits Montreal often. He is quixotic and sociable and sort of takes people under his wing. Big and lumbering with one eye that is slightly sleepy, he wears expensive, loose suits with arty ties and is taken to expansive gesturing. He isn't good-looking but women love him for his charisma and connections. It turns out he knows everyone and everything that is going on; he and his hip, stylish friends allow you into their circle, invite you to their parties, dinners and concerts. Like the Algonquin Round Table of Dorothy Parker, Philip and his hedonist friends do everything together and they do it better than everyone else, including snorting coke, earning high salaries, going to the opera and attending every party that was worth going to. Unfortunately, none of you know that Philip, although highly intelligent, is under the control of cocaine, rather than using it occasionally for fun like the rest of you. He functions very well, manages his high-powered job with no problem, has lots of women, but is secretly spiralling into white-powder perdition.

You will have been in Montreal for a year to the day when you receive a letter from The Philanderer in New Zealand saying he is coming to see you with the intention of reuniting. He misses you. Your blood runs cold (but not cold enough) and you stare at the pages as if they come from a coffin. Your response to his destruction of your love and trust and romantic illusions had been surprisingly decisive. You had really made an effort to become hard in the battle against betrayal and forced yourself with an iron will to erase him from your new world, but now here he is again, looking for more punishment. You have convinced yourself of your own invulnerability, but now you will feel waves of the eviscerating loss of the love that has so wounded you. On and off in the past year you feel the longing for what you thought had been – the good times, the hours of love-making, the complacency of partnership. Sometimes your body betrays you in the sexual memories department, but on the outside you are staunch. So, as is entirely appropriate for someone whose past is catching up with them, you start an affair with a counsellor from work, more to relieve tension and diffuse your fear of seeing The Philanderer than anything else. Rick the Counsellor is a nice, simple boy and far too good and normal for your scarred heart. But the lure of the bad boy is still strong and The Philanderer arrives right on cue.

There he is a few weeks later in the lounge room on Rue Saint François Xavier impressing Bonny, Beth and Shelley with his sexy smile, tight jeans and high-heeled boots. *Oh God*, you think with loathing and panic, *they like him. We'll soon bloody fix that*. You drag them up to the roof, light a joint and say, 'Stop being so nice to him.'

'But he is perfectly charming and so good-looking,' they chorus.

'Of course he's charming. So was Dracula.'

'Oh really, Peta, give the guy a break.'

You go back inside where the girls' boyfriends are amiably chatting away with The Philanderer, the King of Cool. Eventually you have to be alone with him. He slings his things into your bedroom and sits on the bed.

'At least kiss me.'

'I can't.'

'Okay, but you know you're the only woman in the world for me. I have had lots of time to think and I've got other women out of my system.'

'Is that right.'

'Look, I've come all this way. We've got to give it a try.'

'I'm seeing someone else.'

'That's all right. I didn't expect to find you in a hair shirt.'

'Look, you can stay here for a while if you want, but then you'll have to move on.'

'We'll see. If you really don't want me, I'll go to London.'

Every day he tells you he loves you and you are the one and every day you feel yourself vaguely weakening. He probably *does* believe he loves you and you *are* the one because it seems like the right thing to feel at the time. You are invited to Lynne and George's farm for the weekend and drive up with them in their big old Mercedes. In the bucolic setting with your hosts' relaxed hospitality and no pressure on, The Philanderer and you get along well and you manage to modify your rigid stance towards him, while still maintaining a healthy mistrust. You eat huge meals and go for walks and you talk. You tell him you believe you aren't in love with him any more but that you will always love him and maybe in time something could happen. You need time to think and feel again and having sweet Rick doesn't help. But dark clouds are scudding and you don't see them till it is too late. You never find out what it would be like to make love to The Philanderer in a feather bed in the farmhouse because he trumps you. The first night in the country you all go to the pub then crash in various bedrooms in the house.

'Where have you been?' you ask The Philanderer in a sleepy voice the next morning when you wander down for breakfast, assuming he has drunkenly slept in another room.

'I met a girl at the pub and spent the best night in a woman's bed I've had in a long time.'

Everyone stares at you, food midway to their mouths. You instantly snap back into what it feels like to be caught up with him again. You slam your fist down on the table. 'How could you do this to me after coming all this way to get me?'

'Well *you* didn't want me darlin', so I considered myself a free agent.'

'Just because I don't want you absolutely *does not* mean that someone else can have you, you bastard.'

'You're being unreasonable, Peta. You can't have your cake and eat it too.'

'Since when? Where does it say that I can't love you and not love you at the same time? Where? Oh why did I fall for your tricks?'

'But you have Rick, who you parade around in front of me.'

'That is *no* excuse. None whatsoever and I don't parade him. This isn't about Rick and you know it.'

Lynne and George take the devil Philanderer's side because they can't see what he is. You go for a long solitary walk while they have breakfast, make your decision, quietly pack your bag and jump on the first bus back to Montreal. You stare unseeing out the window of the bus in a rancid rage that you have allowed yourself to be fooled. Again.

Back at home the consensus of the wimmin on the rooftop with glasses of wine is that you have no rights over him, but that he has been insensitive to say the least. There was a bit of feminist hair-splitting over that one. Normally the rule is that men are bastards, have no rights and whatever happens, it is their fault and they are bloody lucky to be alive. However, Bonny feels for The Philanderer, probably because she fancies him, and they agree that you should forgive him, so you do on the surface to please them. Mustn't hold a grudge. Needless to say, he gets on a plane to London quite smartly. I'm very sorry to tell you but you do see him again and he does something even worse – a few years later he will ask you to come to London to marry him. You give up your job, your life, your friends, your apartment and your boyfriend, and move to London to find him living with another woman. You'll be pleased to know you are cured after that, but unfortunately will never be able to trust another man again.

When you're a little older you ask yourself if you were liberated or just a slut. The answer is you were liberated. Regrets are for losers and you were extremely lucky to be a twenty-five-year-old in the era of sexual and social revolution, when sex was clean and the air was dirty. Now it's the opposite, so it's just as well you took advantage of it. However, you did take too many risks with hitch-hiking and you are lucky to be alive. You carried around far too many suitcases with far too much in them as you hadn't yet learned to release yourself from the attachment to worldly possessions. It doesn't matter where you are going or for how long – you only need one suitcase. These days you pack one case, take half the stuff out, then lock it. I know you hated nursing and you were a terrible nurse because you were SO in the wrong job, but it was worth graduating because it taught you the meaning of the words 'hard work, discipline and getting dressed while walking to work'. You will realise you were very stupid to stop singing for twenty years – you could have been a professional singer and had a life of hardship, lung disease and cheap hotels. Instead, you go on from age twenty-five to have a life of adventure, romance and French food. And cheap hotels.

When everyone said you would end up old, lonely and tragic because you didn't want children, you were right to trust your instincts that you would have made a frustrated, neurotic mother, and refrain. Good on you for not putting all your eggs in one bastard. If you are happy and loved at twenty-five, the chances are you will be happy and loved at fifty-five right on to ninety-five. Okay, so when the man of your dreams ripped your beating heart out of your chest and threw it away, it took you a while to start breathing again and you became a bit bitter and twisted. Eventually and fortunately you remember that although no one has yet invented a way to take away pain, singing and music come close because they turn pain into beauty. This is when you start singing again.

You and your twenty-five-year-old friends now have no idea of the power you have over men – you are the point of their lives. Use it, don't abuse it. I can't believe how much you ate and never got fat – that changes, trust me. You don't know this yet because you are a drug and alcohol therapist, but food will become your job and your greatest joy – you discover that eating and cooking are the cheapest and easiest way to make yourself and others happy. That happiness is fleeting, thank God, which necessitates frequent repetition. Finally, life will not turn out as you think it will now, when you're young, so it's best to stay open. You can't do everything – your parents will have told you that you are beautiful and can succeed at anything. That's not true – they say that to cut down on psychiatry bills later. You are averagely good-looking, you will never be a brain surgeon, but you will do things and succeed in fields you haven't even thought of yet.

Love, Peta

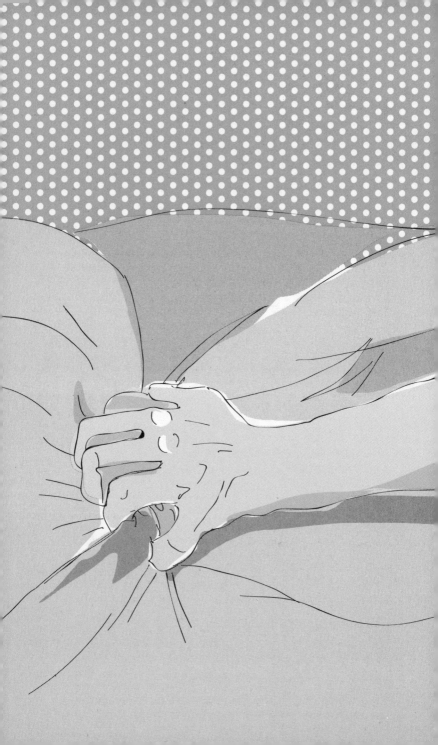

Deactivating the Amygdala

People can have many different kinds
of pleasure. The real one is that for which
they will forsake the others.

Remembrance of Things Past *by Marcel Proust*

'Am I the first man to have made love to you?'
'You might be; your face looks familiar.'

Can we talk here? There are a few questions that I need answered in the interests of personal transformation. Why are we women so multi-orgasmic? Is it evolutionary or is it a happy mistake? Why do many women get tired of making love with their partners after about two years? Why does everyone say women have lower sex drives than men? Why is sex so fantastic at the beginning of a relationship, then often dies till there is no sexual response at all? Is it the woman's fault; is it the man's fault; or is it somehow predestined? If so, why? Is it that *women* don't know about their sexual responses, or are we not meant to be sleeping with the same person long term anyway? Is it that men don't really know anything about women's sexuality? Does having an orgasm make any difference to sex, procreation or to world peace? Why, at some points in our sex lives, do we have to fantasise that we are somewhere else and with someone else other than our long-term partner – maybe we should be with that person? What about people who fantasise about people who look exactly like their own partners? Don't laugh – a lot of women with tall, dark husbands fantasise about tall, dark strangers. Talk about a lack of imagination. Personally, my biggest bedroom fantasy is that the housekeeper will have finally cleaned the blinds properly.

According to a British survey, 42 per cent of women dream of running off with another man; most women never get anywhere near an orgasm with their partner (but have no trouble when masturbating); and 50 per cent of them wish they hadn't married. My friend Suzanne, who really, really wanted to get married, now says she wishes she had enough money to leave her husband, take her two little kids, live in a lovely apartment, work and have fun and be free. She doesn't hate her husband at all, it's just that he's disappointing and she longs for control over her life.

Women are still so controlled and influenced by the

culture they are in that it is difficult to say what a woman's 'true' sexuality is. Take the orgasm in women. Often it is the beginning, not the end, of the story. Often having an orgasm opens up excitement and the woman wishes to continue having sex – so she has more orgasms. Women love taking their time in bed, lolling about, stroking and kissing and touching, laughing, enjoying the feel of skin and the feel of their lover's body. The whole of their lover's body, that is. Women who desire men like to feel the entire length of a man's body against theirs. There is nothing worse for a woman than to have a man approach her too quickly and 'cut to the chase' without any sensual preamble. It feels like an attack; it is sexually meaningless. We need context, communication and sweetness. Actually most humans do but, inexplicably, men often want to bypass this – it can't be satisfying for them either. Surely. If they want to have swift sex with something warm, pliable and moist, why don't they just go and buy some liver? It worked for Portnoy. Poetry aside, what women need most to enjoy sex and have an orgasm is the occurrence of a neurological change in the brain.

To relax enough to have an orgasm, the amygdala, the part of the brain responsible for your anxiety, fear and memory of emotional reactions, must be deactivated. The amygdala is found in my favourite section of the brain – the dog brain or limbic system. In my book on men, *Just in Time to be Too Late*, I talk about our three brains: the original, primitive lizard brain located at the base of the neck; the second, more sophisticated dog or limbic brain sitting on top of the lizard brain; and the huge human brain or neocortex, which sits on top of that and owns most of your skull's real estate. The need to turn off the amygdala in order to orgasm is probably why it takes some women ten times longer than it does most men. The man doesn't have to turn anything off – he just goes for it. How do you turn the amygdala off? It happens automatically when you are turned on sexually, but it can take a while to stop worrying about whether the door is locked, whether your butt is still huge, and whether or not you trust this person anyway. In his book *The Female Orgasm*, psychologist Seymour Fisher says that women who have difficulty orgasming with a man are afraid, on a deep level, of desertion (back to the trust issue). He says the man's technique is actually not that important and the woman's unwillingness to 'let go' goes back to how she feels about her father. If she trusted him not to leave her, she will be more likely to trust the man she is in bed with.

Have you ever felt there is a direct line from your pelvis to your brain? You're right – there is. Have you ever felt that your attraction to a person is *literally* electrochemical and has nothing to do with conscious decision-making? You're right – it is. There *is* a direct line straight from the nerves in the clitoris to the pleasure centre in the brain. All going well, when you are turned on, electrochemical waves trigger powerful drugs like endorphins and oxytocin, which make you feel gooey and happy. Here's a tip for any man who has ever asked the extremely annoying, 'Did you come?' First, don't ask it – do you live in a cave? Second, if a woman comes she has a flushed face and neck, she is very calm and happy, and her inner thighs may be trembling. Okay? Clear enough? The female orgasm is a completely different deal from the male one. The clitoris is not a mini penis. An orgasm comes from the stimulation of the opening and outer third of the vagina, the urethra and the clitoris, all of which are connected by blood vessels and nerves. There is no such thing as a vaginal as opposed to clitoral orgasm – it takes the three areas of the whole organ to do the job.

Women can enjoy sex, get pregnant, polish their nails and give birth without having an orgasm, so what role does it play in evolutionary terms? There are many theories. As many as twenty. The predominant one is that orgasm in women is connected to fertility. The spasms from orgasms cause the uterus to sort of 'suck up' sperm, ensuring a greater chance of conception. Supposedly, if you orgasm at the same time as ejaculation or within half an hour afterwards, you conserve more sperm. My lesbian friends have told me that when they were using the turkey baster system for artificial insemination they always masturbated to orgasm at the same time or soon afterwards. This reminds me. I worked for several years for a gynaecologist in Vancouver who specialised in fertility treatment and artificial insemination. I, Nurse Peta, used to run across the road to the medical students' secret drop-off place, pick up the warm tube of semen, and run back to the clinic where the patient would be waiting virtuously with her knees pointing to God. Who says life can't be exciting? If the woman was being inseminated by her own husband, I would usher him into a room in the clinic with a container and some *Playboy* magazines. It was very hard not to knock on the door and ask if I could help – not everyone thought that was funny.

On the television series *The Great Sperm Race*, it was explained in thrilling detail that the orgasm and conception theory was the way to go. Dr Allan Pacey, a senior lecturer in andrology at Sheffield University, says that if a couple is seriously trying to conceive, they should make love with great passion and wild abandon as if they had only met yesterday. If you are having what he calls 'gourmet sex' rather than 'we're-trying-to-conceive sex', which can be really boring and routine, you are much more likely to hit the jackpot. Here's why: when a man delivers a big fat outrageous ejaculation he shoots out about 500 million sperm; when it's just a humdrum, routine offload he has about half that. Even five more minutes of super-duper foreplay can increase the sperm count by 25 million, and those wee guys are superior, tip-top, healthy sperm too! I *know* – that's what I thought. The more turned-on the man is, the more likely it is he will be ejaculating sperm from deep within the testicle.

But wait, there's more. In gourmet sex the woman is probably going to have a big fat outrageous orgasm too.

The muscular contractions are so intense during the changes in pressure that her body is experiencing, that sperm is sucked into her cervix and thence to the tabernacle of the womb, where all those millions of sperm only have to penetrate one of her eggs. It's absolutely amazing really. I can hear the music.

An osteopath told me one of the other effects of a huge sperm count from a big ejaculation is that, as most of them don't even get past the cervix, they act as 'guards' against the next invasion of sperm, which might not be theirs. Thus the rejects actually protect paternity. I know you want to know if the same goes for animals, so I will tell you. Farmers in Denmark masturbate sows while they are being artificially inseminated, which apparently results in a 6 per cent higher fertility rate. Quite a lot of unpleasant effort for little payback, you might think. You may think that's disgusting, but the Danish government doesn't: they organise courses to show farmers how to do it. This could never happen in a country like New Zealand, a place where the men are men and the sheep are nervous. For research purposes I got talking to an artificial inseminator of cows in Ireland who told me New Zealand semen is of very high quality, a piece of unnecessary information guaranteed to put me off my supper. You and I probably wouldn't use the quality of our sperm as a chat-up line, but there you go – the charm of country people. When he wasn't tricking bulls into thinking they were doing the wild thing with a comely heifer, this inseminator played the squeeze box (no pun intended) to keep himself sane. I should think you'd need something.

Another theory about female orgasms is that women only orgasm during intercourse with certain favoured men – not all men – thus performing a sort of genetic selection. That is, if he's handsome, strong and adept, she will have an orgasm with him and those characteristics of his may be passed on to their progeny. Another theory is the mistake theory: the clitoris is a 'leftover' from early embryonic development. Just as males have nipples they don't need, females have tissue similar to a penis that serves no purpose other than to generate pleasure. It's a bliss node, not a delivery device. All foetuses are 'female' to start off with. At about six to eight weeks, if the embryo is to become male, it is 'washed' in testosterone and turns into a boy. Nerve pathways are laid down for orgasms in boys, some of which are retained if the foetus stays female. Another hypothesis – a worrying one – suggests that in evolutionary terms the female orgasm is disappearing, which is why it is so irregular and unpredictable.

Women have been told for a long time that they are supposed to be having orgasms during intercourse and they feel inadequate when they don't achieve this. Men have been taught to expect an orgasm from a woman and when it doesn't happen, they feel inadequate. But what if it's probably not meant to happen with some women? What if it really does serve no reproductive service other than having a really good time? What if you can have a really good time and not orgasm? It is a fact that many women report being very happy with sex and enjoying it without orgasm, just as many orgasmic women say they don't particularly enjoy sex. You don't have to have an orgasm to enjoy sex. The proof is that you orgasm when you masturbate, but you're not having sex are you – you're playing poker with one hand. The fact is no one actually knows why some people orgasm and some people don't. There is only one orgasm and it is clitoral. The sure-fire way to have an orgasm with a man is if he successfully stimulates the clitoris with his fingers or tongue, or if you are in a position where the penis is rubbing against the clitoris during penetration. You can imagine how hit and miss this is – I'm getting a nose bleed just thinking about it. And then there's the complication of why a woman isn't enjoying sex with a man. Usually it's rage. It is very common to withhold sex out of anger, or to use it as a bargaining tool. I knew a woman who hated performing oral sex on her husband. The poor guy was practically on *his* knees – begging. So she would exchange a blow-job for a home appliance. She would tell us these stories till the tears ran down our faces. One time, she got a washing machine for a blow-job. Call me old-fashioned, but a washing machine for a blow-job is a bloody good deal. Seriously, though, the price women pay for withholding sex is the loss of genuine excitement and romance.

Because the brain is the most powerful sex organ we have, people can also have dream orgasms – what my friends call snorgasms, where they wake up coming, having not touched or been touched. My editor was fascinated by the term snorgasm, so I looked it up and it turns out to have other meanings and every person who uses the term thinks they have made it up. It can mean a boring love-making experience; a very deep calm sleep; the sharp snoring sound a woman sometimes makes when orgasming; falling asleep on the job; a sneeze; preferring sleep to sex; a wet dream; a very loud explosive snore which wakes the snorer. The most interesting one I found was related to a hormonal function associated with fertility called 'mittelschmerz'. Mittelschmerz means 'middle pain' and refers to the pelvic discomfort some women experience when ovulating. The pain probably comes from contractions in either the ovary and its ligaments, or the fallopian tube. Sometimes at mittelschmerz the vulva may also swell. There is a theory that snorgasms can happen at the same time as these contractions, mimicking the vaginal contractions in orgasm and also, handily, dulling the pain once you wake up. Boys also have this but it's associated with the testes lining wearing off every month – who knew? Who needed to? The mittelschmerz story was in the past associated with the myth of the incubus, a male demon who came in the night and lay upon women, giving them unconscious orgasms (if they were lucky). The female version was the succubus, who lay on men. When the man awoke he had semen on him, which people in medieval times thought was the gift of the succubus.

I like the orgasm-in-your-sleep version of snorgasm. My friend Michele woke up in the night recently and found her husband staring at her. She asked him what he was doing and he replied that he was watching to see if she could snorgasm. Now all my friends want one and feel like underachievers if it doesn't happen. All I can say is, it's like maturing cheese – it won't happen overnight but it will happen.

• • •

Why do people masturbate all the time, basically from childhood, and how come they mostly discover it all by themselves without anyone ever mentioning it? Why would a child masturbate? Because it feels good, that's why. All children fiddle with themselves till it feels good. They only stop because the parent takes the child's hand away and tells it not to be dirty. Happily, most of us persist. I suppose you could argue that once the woman becomes an adult, the pleasure of masturbating leads her to want to have sex. Some female monkeys have orgasms and scientists have suggested this ability developed to protect their babies from attack by the males. Here's the reasoning: in some primates the mortality rate of babies is very high because the males will kill any baby which is not their own. They don't kill the babies of females with whom they have done the wild thing. The female monkey likes having orgasms (through clitoral stimulation), so she keeps mating with lots and lots of males so no one knows who the father is. That way, the males won't kill because they can't identify their baby. Or, alternatively, if the male has associations of mutual pleasure with the female, he will look on her children more kindly. The most outrageous sex addict primates are the bonobo monkeys, which are said to be the closest relative to humans. The bonobos have a matriarchal society. The females have breasts similar to humans, not flat like chimpanzees', and their faces are different from each other, as human faces are. Both sexes believe in love not war and when confronted with a violent or conflict-ridden situation, will resolve it by having sex. They have sex face to face, put their arms around each other, kiss and masturbate. The males hardly ever kill the babies. I love bonobos.

All this doesn't answer the question of multiple orgasm – and I haven't even got onto the subject of female ejaculation yet. In my book on women, *Can We Help It If We're Fabulous?*, this subject is broached. Female ejaculation is not really ejaculation and doesn't come from the clitoris. It is clear fluid that spurts in tiny amounts from ducts near the opening of the urethra during orgasm. Some say it doesn't exist and some say it happens very rarely. As for the fact that women can orgasm over and over again, one after the other with short spaces in between: maybe. If *one* feels good – six will feel better! Actually, both male and female children can multiple orgasm. The boy achieves it because he is not ejaculating, but when he reaches maturity and male hormones kick in it becomes much harder to pull this off. The theory is that women can do it because they don't ejaculate. Another thing – why is a woman's orgasm longer than a man's and seemingly more intense? I don't know, but I'm grateful. And one more thing – orgasms are good for your cardiovascular health, not to mention your mental health. So, if you don't have someone to make love with, make sure you look after yourself. Sex, they say, is like poker: if you don't have a good partner, you had better have a good hand. By the way, female alligators also have clitorises.

• • •

A danger is that women begin to think that truly expressing female sexual behaviour means copying or being like men. This is akin to what happened to women in the 1980s in business, when they thought that competing with men in the workplace meant assuming dominant, left-brain, male behaviour like logic and analysis, when in fact, using typical right-brain female traits like co-operation and creativity worked much better. Women who fake orgasms to please men offer a perfect example of unhelpful and false sexual behaviour. No wonder men are confused – we lie to them constantly with our bodies. The way forward is to experience true female passion, find out what that is and don't settle for less. Don't do anything you don't want to do, don't sleep with men who just want to cut to the chase, and stick to that decision. Women who dress in a grossly provocative way, strip, get drunk and are sexually aggressive either have a hormone imbalance (too much testosterone) or are behaving in a masculinised way because they think that's what being liberated means. I know a woman like this. Middle age has stripped her of oestrogen and progesterone, leaving her with relatively too much testosterone and turning her into a grotesque desperado who puts her hands on men's genitals and exposes herself. When a woman behaves this way, what are men to think? A normal, kind man feels sorry for her disconnection from her true self; a dumb man thinks that is what she wants. If women keep letting men short-change them and expect them to assume a male version of sexuality, they are perpetuating a cycle of lies in which everyone is short-changed.

Most women don't think it's sexy to be approached too quickly; they don't think it's sexy to be instantly reduced to a cunt; they don't think it's sexy for men to expose themselves. True female sexuality is a sensual, vibrant thing like a cello note, which involves being in control. It lies in general sexiness, unfolding, playing, not isolating body parts. Women are not about body parts at all. Examples of truly sexy goddesses are Scarlett Johansson, Sophia Loren, Penélope Cruz, Annette Bening, Michelle Obama, Audrey Hepburn and every top Indian actress.

A good way to discover your female sexuality is to read good female writers writing on sex. Women such as Anaïs Nin, Erica Jong, Shere Hite. I find it impossible to write good sex scenes because I can't help either laughing or remembering the gynaecology ward when I was a nurse. If you haven't had a lot of sexual experience, get some, while keeping in mind honesty, openness, a sense of humour and a condom.

• • •

Testosterone is the sex hormone in both men and women – we both have it and we both need it. Men need it for the maintenance of a masculine appearance, to get an erection, for mental and physical vitality, and to play dick-head football games. Women need it for bone density, libido, muscle mass and becoming Russian astronauts. A long time ago, researchers realised that if you give people testosterone therapy, their libido will revive. In *Can We Help It If We're Fabulous?* I recount the time I talked an endocrinologist into injecting me with a small dose of testosterone. I didn't want it for libido reasons; I wanted it for the typical positive male traits like strength, focus, energy, visual and spatial skills and being less emotional. Don't even start me on what happened. Within a few days I turned into a nineteen-year-old boy and couldn't think about anything but sex. I was permanently horny and saw no signs of increased strength, better eyesight or anything resembling focus. My sole focus was sex; it was very distracting and I couldn't wait for the effect to wear off so I could get on with my work.

● ● ●

To better understand women's sexuality, I drove out of town to visit a sex therapist, who lives in the bush in a gingerbread house. It was winter. We sat outside with heaters on and talked about the beautiful thing. Kathryn Barriball is a psychotherapist who has specialised in sex and sex-abuse counselling for many years. I asked her if I was right to suppose that most women are like me in terms of their sexuality. If I talk about myself, I am talking about all women. How different can we be?

KB: Yes. I used to think that too, but guess what – not all women are the same and not all men are the same either. Also, what I have realised over my years of counselling is that the gender gap is not as wide as I had assumed it was – there's more similarity than difference. So much of our sexuality is to do with societal messages and upbringing.

PM: So, if you were counselling someone in Nairobi, they might be coming to you with completely different problems?

KB: Yeah. Well, I don't see anyone as a problem unless they are abusive, which is another story. Most of my clients come as couples and it's usually because there is a discrepancy between them. It's not usually that one wants more or less sex than the other; it's simply that they're not getting a good match together. You would maybe think that men would present saying their wife doesn't want to have sex as often as they do, but in my experience it is quite often the other way round. Sexual desire is motivated by three things: your hormones, your head and your heart. I haven't yet come across a diagnosis of hormonal deficiency (e.g. testosterone) but I do get that checked out.

PM: I read about some research the other day in which people were wired up for sexual tests. They had photos and videos of various sexual activities put in front of them and were asked what turned them on and what didn't. Surprisingly often, the women said they weren't turned on by a photo at all, but the wiring showed sexual arousal which they were completely unaware of.

KB: That doesn't surprise me at all. I think to a large extent we are unaware of our true sexual responses because of the imposition of culture, education, et cetera. Also, I think that with a man it's quite obvious if he's aroused because his penis changes, but with a woman the arousal could be so subtle that she's not even aware of it. Most people are not that tuned in to the little things. One of the standard techniques I use for people with low desire is to get them to be aware of 'simmering', noticing the lower level, observing little thoughts or scenes that turn you on during the day. Then you can go home and see if your partner is interested in playing. Or send him a suggestive text so you set him up during the day – keeping the arousal simmering.

PM: Yes, but why *do* we lose our desire after a few years when we couldn't keep our hands, and the rest, off each other at the beginning? And I'm not even talking children, hormones, tiredness or anything else. Why would two people in, say, their thirties, with no children, no stress, who love each other, go off sex?

KB: Some couples do have a great long-term sex life, but it's true that a lot don't. The main problem, which always amazes me, is that even really together, intelligent people don't talk about sex with each other. You can't make assumptions. What turned your partner on five years ago might not turn them on now – and your conditions for arousal change too. Also, people are on drugs when they first meet – they're flooded with oxytocin and endorphins. But like any drug, the effects are not going to last forever – they can't, you would be exhausted and never get anything done. Nothing stays the same with humans – if you had spinach every night for dinner you'd get sick of that too. The great feeling you get from gambling recedes so you have to gamble more and more and take bigger and bigger risks; the body gets used to sleeping pills and you have to take larger doses. Love needs closeness, but passion needs distance, so in your relationship you both have to be responsible for your own needs. It is your job to attend to your sexual needs and let your partner know what they are.

PM: So really it all comes back to communication. People find it embarrassing to say what they want; they think their partner should be observant and sense what pleases them. They also don't want him to think they're weird or something. We have sex in our faces all day in the media but apparently we still don't know how to have it. The author of the updated *The Joy of Sex* says people need the book now more than they ever did.

KB: There is innate sexual desire and subjective sexual desire. Innate is something that just hits you spontaneously, like when you first meet;

subjective is when you work up to it. When the innate stuff wears off, people think it's all over, but it's not. They give up too easily – they're just moving on to the next stage. This is where you have to build the head and the heart up, which I mentioned before, to keep the desire going. In regards to sex after menopause, a really good book to read is *The Secret Pleasures of Menopause* by Dr Christiane Northrup.

PM: Why are women multi-orgasmic and men aren't?

KB: No reason I know of except to have pleasure. Also, not all women are multi-orgasmic either and some men are, but it's unusual because by the process of ejaculation, they need a refractory period. Women don't have this incredible build-up of energy and blood that they have to recover from. A lot of women are incapable of having another orgasm so soon after the first because they can't be touched.

PM: And what about this business of men now telling us they sometimes ejaculate without orgasm and orgasm without ejaculating? Have they been faking or what? We're supposed to be the fakers – do they have to move in on our territory? Are we all faking? What a bloody minefield.

KB: You're right and that is why I say I don't

believe there is such a thing as female or male sexual nature. We are all influenced by the media version of what sex and love is supposed to be. All love movies are based on the first stage of a relationship – they never move out of that, so people learn very young that they are supposed to have simultaneous orgasm, multi-orgasm and hot sex forever. In reality very few people do any of those things and so feel there is something wrong with them when they don't. We think sex has to correlate with orgasm – it doesn't. And we think sex means penetration – it doesn't. People restrict themselves to a really narrow repertoire, but there are many, many sexual ways to have fun. We set ourselves up for completely unnecessary failure.

PM: If a couple has not had sex for years, can they get their mojo back again?

KB: Yes. I have seen that happen with people in my care. It's tough, though. The longer it's been, the harder it is to get it back because you grow apart in so many other ways. They would really only successfully get it on again if they opened up to a lot of other stuff – the old communication thing again. If a couple can achieve this, the growth potential is enormous.

PM: Talk to me about Viagra.

KB: I'm not too thrilled with Viagra. I think it's

okay as a temporary solution. It gives a man confidence to do whatever else he has to do to get his sexuality back. What I hear from my colleagues is that women are really over Viagra. Slowing down sexually is a developmental thing in human lifespan and we should celebrate and enjoy that – it's not about being like a teenager. You're in no hurry. You don't have to have a great big dick every time.

PM: Do you know what I think? I think it's a bloody conspiracy orchestrated by the media to make us buy into a product – the product of being perfect.

KB: Yes, and we all have stunted emotional growth – we're all like teenagers. I think people are growing up much more slowly these days. The good thing is we now live much longer and we have prioritised pleasure in our lives. You and I were both brought up Catholic – we were taught that we weren't put on this Earth to enjoy ourselves . . .

PM: Wow – we have adjusted really well.

I thought Kathryn's advice was exceptionally helpful and felt like putting it up on my fridge, but I still didn't feel I had got to the crux of the matter: that is, my theory that women would be a lot more sexually active with a lot more partners if society permitted it. So I sat down and reread my copy of *The Female Brain* by Louann Brizendine. She talks about the myth of female fidelity and says women are no more programmed to be faithful than they are to fly to the moon. We already know that at least 10 per cent of fathers are not genetically related to some of their children, and that they are unaware of this. As far as they are concerned, they are the father and have no reason to think otherwise. Why do married women who are happy with their husbands sleep with another man, conceive a child, give birth to the child and then conceal it forever? According to genetic studies, the woman is more likely to have a giant orgasm with another, usually better-looking, more sexy man, thus ensuring reproduction. She may start faking orgasms with her safe, not-so-sexy husband, to trick him into thinking she's satisfied while having real ones with her lover.

It seems the female orgasm might be extremely selective, devious and sly in a subconscious way. The woman wants to marry the safe, nice man but wants to have sex with Tarzan. Brizendine maintains that women are designed to keep their sexual options open for top-quality sperm (in a genetic way). I knew it! It has always seemed to me that women need a lot more variety than men, rather than the other way round. And we need less sex than men, but sex of a higher quality. A man can sleep with the same woman forever and never stray. True. Meanwhile, that woman went mad about thirty years ago and has been pretending ever since – to keep the peace. Researcher Shere Hite, who famously wrote *The Hite Report*, says sex is not so much a biological as a cultural institution; that a society institutes its own meaning for sex to suit reproductive requirements, not intuitive or natural requirements. This idea is interesting because it supposes the meaning of sex can change and should be allowed to change. We women have already culturally transformed how we wish to express our sexuality and it will be up to us to continue, elegantly and confidently, to express our freedom and 'true' selves.

Eat, Sing, Love

> Woman is like a fruit which will only yield
> its fragrance when rubbed by the hands.
> Take for example basil: unless it is warmed
> by the fingers, it emits no perfume. And do
> you know that unless amber is warmed and
> manipulated it retains its aroma within?
>
> The Perfumed Garden of Sensual Delight
> *by Muhammad ibn Muhammad al-Nafzawi*

Food, music and love are all profoundly transformative. When I was in my twenties I redecorated entire households every six months, taught hopeless flatmates to cook and clean, threw huge dinner parties and cooked, cooked, cooked. This was the same as saying loved, loved, loved. Eating and loving made me and everyone else happy and was a form of therapy, transforming our lives from the mundane to the sublime – if only for half an hour.

Desire drives us to seek out both food and love, and both are a really cheap way to achieve transformation without meditating or medicating. Making bread, for example, gives you so much pleasure that you can just pick up the phone and cancel that appointment with the shrink – you don't need to share your noxious feelings after all. The first thing you do when you come out of the womb, after screaming your head off in fright, is eat. You drink your mother's loving milk and from then on, never stop eating and loving (or looking for it). In her magical book *Like Water for Chocolate*, Laura Esquivel tells us that her heroine, Tita, made luscious recipes that transformed people from disliking each other to wanting to make love.

We swim in music like fish swim in water and our hunger for it seems to have no limits. Music and singing transform and enhance our moods by the release of the love hormone oxytocin. Music provides instant access to emotional states in a way no other form of communication can, and studies have shown that we are actually physically affected by music and that the effect is different in everyone. How is it that we manage to leave out a lot in singing, sing in a foreign language, or have no personal experience of the topic at hand, but can still be transformed and moved by a song? There is also the complicity between a singer or musician and their audience – like love, the act requires a giver and a receiver. The audience must graciously give of themselves, be attentive and actively give into the seduction of the song. No one has yet invented a way to take away pain, but singing comes close. Music turns grief into beauty. Incidentally karaoke, which means 'empty orchestra', is not transformative – it's just God's way of telling you you've drunk too much.

Speaking of alcohol, MRI scans of people in love show that their brains look the same as those of people addicted to drugs or alcohol. When two people meet and are attracted to each other, an arsenal of powerful chemicals is released by the brain: dopamine, norepinephrine and heavenly serotonin. Talk about a transformation! In this form of euphoric psychosis we go from normal human being to love addict in days, and in the first phase of love we go blind, become deaf and stop eating. If the person had two heads we wouldn't notice, so wondrous and perfect do they seem. The Muslim poet Rumi said: 'Lovers don't finally meet somewhere – they're in each other all along.' The drugs eventually wear off to ensure that we can get things done, but if they didn't occur, there would be no sexual attraction, no madly falling in love and no one would sing and dance and eat, which is what this story is all about.

• • •

It's a weekend in south-west France. I wake up on Saturday morning on the floor, next to a dead fire, to the sound of birds chirping and Gabriel softly snoring. I look at him and his hair sticking straight up and feel a flutter in my chest

– in the area I assume to be where my heart is. A lifetime of being outdoors and drinking lots of wine shows in one or two deeply etched lines around his eyes and the sides of his mouth. The room has an open-beamed ceiling, long, Provençal-style dining table and antique dresser with ribbons attached to the keys. Ducks are whispering and chattering and water is running somewhere. After lying there for a while I move to get up. The minute I move, Gabriel, eyes still shut, grabs my arm.

'Où vas-tu?'

'Where's the bathroom?'

'Upstairs. Promise you'll come back before lunch.'

'Mmm. The choice between spending the morning in the bathroom and spending it on a cold floor is hard but . . . promise.'

I climb the narrow stairs lined with engraved mirrors and wander along a short, stone-tiled corridor with false, painted doors obviously found at the flea-market and stuck onto the walls. I poke my head into two bedrooms then find the bathroom with skylight and old-fashioned bathtub. While I'm up there I can't resist looking around. The bedrooms are full of paintings, dried flowers and bric-a-brac, and have heavy, brocade rugs over the windows instead of curtains. When I get downstairs again, Gabriel has lit the fire to take the chill off the morning, and I slip quietly under the huge duvet to join him.

We laugh and make love and laugh and make love. Everything goes wrong, everything goes right. I am everyone he has ever loved and he is everyone I have ever loved. He admires my kneecaps, my hands, my lips, my hips, my dips – in fact every dip in my body is attended to. I kiss him so fiercely that he jerks and flings his arm out into the fire, which dislodges a log and sends sparks exploding onto us. We both scream, a dog outside begins barking and scratching at the door and the ducks start up. He throws his boots at the door as I lie on top of him, covering his body with my own, covering him with my hair, covering him with my love. The duvet starts smouldering, we pour a glass of water on it and keep kissing as if we're about to miss the last train. He smells of sweet fresh sweat, wood and whatever perfumed soap he has laundered his sheets in. I'm thinking if we don't mingle soon the whole place will burn down and my heart and soul with it. We are drenched, the duvet is drenched, the animals are in a sympathetic frenzy, we are in another country, another world, our hearts thumping in unison, doing the one thing that really makes the world go round.

Gabriel's house is a small, seventeenth-century, two-storeyed building that slopes in all directions due to its age and the fact that he can't afford to fix it up. I love it as it is and wouldn't change one single crack in the paint, one split beam, one windy window.

'I bought this house cheaply because it was in bad condition and places in these villages don't cost much anyway, although there are so many bloody English buying down here now, the prices are being pushed up,' he explains as he moves around the kitchen making breakfast. There are no kettles or teapots in your average French kitchen because they don't drink tea, so if you want a cuppa you have to boil water in a pot and put a tea bag in a cup. It's all very sauvage. The cupboards in this lovely house are painted faded watermelon pink and the TV is hidden in an old cabinet painted with a cracked Art Deco design. An old chandelier with pink candles in it hangs over the table and every room is stuffed full of antique chairs, statues, paintings, little lamps and artifacts like old lace-makers, old puppets, old books.

'My family and I spend a lot of time at antique fairs and marchés aux puces,' Gabriel tells me. 'Nothing in here cost anything except the paintings, and the basement is full of even more stuff. Sometimes I lose entire cases of wine I've put down there because I can't find them. If it was ever emptied out, I would probably end up being a wealthy man.'

I wrap the sheet around myself and wander out into the brilliantly sunny day through the door that leads from the dining room to a terrace at the back of the house. High wisteria-laden walls ensure complete privacy and yellow roses and hollyhocks grow out of the spaces between the cobblestones. This terrace has a three-tiered, overgrown garden full of berry bushes and wild, old-fashioned roses that goes straight down to the river Dronne.

I am so happy I feel delirious wandering around in the

first bare feet of the season and smelling of Gabriel and love. I consider never washing again – for thirty seconds. I'm drawn into the kitchen by smells of toast and warm croissants and freshly ground coffee. This kitchen has walls completely covered by antique cooking implements. There's an old-fashioned sink and no dishwasher. On a window shelf is a crock of home-made red wine vinegar and the kitchen table is laden with bottles of home-made jam, figs in eau-de-vie and stewed prunes. I look at them longingly, then look at Gabriel with the faintest flicker of lust, then drag my mind back to the food. Food, love, food, love. How's a girl to choose?

'Where did these come from, Gabriel? You're surely not going to tell me you do bottling in your spare time,' I say, unwrapping my sheet and rewrapping him in it with me.

'No, Maman did them. She does hundreds in the summer. This is all that's left over from last summer and if you look out the window you'll see the fig tree they came from. Unfortunately we've missed the Friday market, which is one of the best in the area, but I'll take you to another one in Périgueux – it's only about thirty kilometres from here,' he replies, hugging me and kissing my neck and rubbing his stubble all over my face.

'Are we having some of Maman's jam with our toast?'

'Oui, oui, évidemment,' he says, unwrapping himself. 'Right, you grab this tray and I'll bring the other stuff out. I'm afraid the croissants are yesterday's but we can dunk them in the coffee.'

We plonk our feast down on the rusty white table, Gabriel throws open the peeling shutters and we sit there sipping our strong coffee and smearing buttery croissants all over our lips and chins. He licks the crumbs off my face and I lick the crumbs off his. You look after me, I'll look after you. You heal my wounds, I'll heal yours. Healing by food; healing by love. When a person cooks they produce very intense personal energy, and when they prepare food with this energy, as well as love, those qualities are transferred to the people who eat it. As usual, my decision about Gabriel is already made. Making love to him is simply my way of giving him permission to fall in love with me. He puts his feet up on my thighs and stares at me with bedroom eyes.

By the time we make love again, shower, get dressed, tidy up the dining room and do the dishes, it's eleven o'clock and there's little time left to go to the Saturday market. We jump in the car and drive at breakneck speed through serene and lustrous green land and the narrow, winding roads of tiny villages to the bustling town of Périgueux. The sun filters through the poplars making everything romantic and exotic. I've never been this far south; in fact I've hardly ever been out of Paris in the two years I've been in France, so all this bucolic overkill is opium to my senses. I love the smell of markets and always stick my nose right into everything. Farmers, fishmongers selling live fish, clothes traffickers and cheese traders overflowing. They're used to les Anglaises folles here in the Dordogne, so I get away with a lot more than I do at a Paris market in terms of cheeky repartee with the stall-holders. A lot of them know Gabriel and stare closely at me, wondering just what our connection is.

The big products here are the famous goose and duck foie gras and those jet-black rocks of earthy ecstasy – truffles. The pale, fattened livers are lined up in rows on a refrigerated bench looking like slabs of butter. We find an old woman, sharp as a snake, not to be separated from her truffles without emptying our wallets and I leave Gabriel to negotiate. It's a very extravagant buy but we'll make one little truffle the size of a walnut last a long time by putting it in with the eggs and slicing it very finely so that we find fungi heaven in every meal – pasta with truffles, scrambled eggs with truffles, sliced potatoes with truffles. Further down the market I find mountains of walnuts, huge tables of rye and sourdough bread, baskets of sorrel, regional charcuterie and goat cheeses with crazy names like Chabichou, Couhé-vérac wrapped in chestnut leaves and La-Mothe-Saint-Héraye. I buy all these cheeses simply to reward them for having great names. Just as I finger a bottle of walnut oil I feel Gabriel's closeness.

'Peta,' he says, putting the oil back, 'we can get much better oil from my friends at Champagne-de-Belair. Have you seen everything you want to see? I want to buy some wine, then we can have a coffee and go home.'

'No, no, no, I haven't seen everything. Shall we buy some foie gras? I want to lie down under these tables and stay here for the rest of my life,' I cry, 'and just in case I get peckish, I've bought some bread, cheese and pâté.'

He grabs my arm and marches me towards the wine shop on the edge of the market. 'The market's not going away, Peta. It'll be here next time you come and it'll be here after you die.'

I stop, dig my fingers into his beloved arm and stare at him intently. People are swirling around us. Two lovers looking each other straight in the eye. 'Die? I'm going to live forever and Gabriel, do you think there'll be a next time?'

He puts down his basket full of vegetables, brushes the hair out of my eyes and says, very close to my nose, 'I hope I never come to this market again without you, I hope the geese in the Dordogne refuse to be force-fed unless by your hands, I hope to be crushed by an army of marauding Mongols before I look at another woman, I hope your goat cheese that is at this very moment enjoying synthesis with my shirt will stain it permanently in memory of you.'

'Aaah,' I groan, pulling away from him, 'shall I lick it off?'

'Yes, lick it off, lick it off,' says a plummy English voice behind me. I turn around to see a very pretty girl with long, honey-blonde hair and hazel eyes laughing at us.

Five minutes later we're seated at the Café du Marché drinking double espressos with Gabriel's older brother, Claude, and his English girlfriend, India. Claude is much straighter-looking than Gabriel, but they seem to have an

identical temperament. Their mannerisms are the same –
expansiveness, confidence, humour and verbal velocity,
but the brother's face is less interesting, more harmonious,
more ordinary. They are sort of wary of each other but
also friendly – the way things often are with siblings.
You may wish to strangle family, but blood is still thicker
than water. India is delightful, open, talkative, and I
can't stop staring at her. She's that pretty. We immediately enter into intimate conversation, blocking out the
other two. The warmth of the spring sunshine as we all
sit around the café table sipping and talking acts like a
shower of gold dust.

'What's that musky smell?' I ask, wrinkling my nose and
looking around.

'It'll be the truffle,' replies Gabriel. 'The aroma of a truffle
is extraordinarily pervasive, you know.'

'One small truffle?' I marvel, rooting around in his
basket to have a look. 'It's wrapped in screeds of paper at
the bottom of your bag. I can hardly believe that.'

Claude looks at Gabriel scathingly. 'You paid for a
truffle? Why didn't you just go out and look for one? You
must really be besotted to buy her a truffle.'

'Ta gueule. I haven't got all day to ferret around for
truffles, idiot. We're only here for the weekend and anyway
we're leaving. Can't waste the day on you.'

On the way back to Brantome we stop off for the walnut
oil. Gabriel tells me there used to be lots of walnut mills in
the area but this is the only one left now and it's 700 years

old. We go for a little tour of the mill, which is in repose as it's not the season. I'm amazed to see that the press is just an old-fashioned machine. Nearby is the old cauldron that heats up the walnuts over a wood fire before they are pressed. Gabriel goes back to the car to get a wine bottle and cork.

'I always bring my own bottle to get refilled and I much prefer to buy it here as it's cheaper and fresher than at the market. Smell the cork and you'll get an idea of what it smells like around here when Marcel's pressing in the autumn – you can inhale walnuts for miles. It's quite strong so you only use a little at a time in salads or sprinkled over cooked food.'

By now it's well and truly time to eat again, but I notice that Gabriel drives past the village.

'Where are we going?'

'On va aller aux fraises.'

'But it's not strawberry season.'

He laughs. 'Don't you know what that means?'

'No, tell me.'

'It's an old south-west expression. To take someone walking in the woods is like going down lover's lane. You go strawberry picking with a woman for only one reason.'

'Oh, right then, let's go.'

After the strawberry-picking session, which happily combines at least a thousand honey-dripping kisses, grass stains on clothes, twigs in hair (adding artfully to the pre-existing tangle), we stumble wobbly-legged back to the car.

On Sunday we go to Dodo's recording studio in Périgueux to record some music another friend has written for the rock opera that is the project of his life. Dodo (Daniel) and Gabriel are old friends and they record a lot, in part because they love music but also to hang out together and talk rubbish. Gabriel finds and re-records old songs and music of the region as well as jazz. This project is exceptional in that rock operas are not really his thing, but he's helping his friend Emmanuel out of the goodness of his heart. Other friends come and go with no obvious purpose in life. Every so often in the dark, fetid studio Gabriel shouts 'ALL NON-ESSENTIALS OUT' with great authority and everyone leaves except him, Emmanuel, Dodo and eighty thousand francs worth of artificial music. Wires and cords are everywhere, trailing from computers, keyboards, recording equipment and microphones. Other non-essential friends hang out in the antechamber sucking on cigarettes and telling lies about what they did the night before.

Dodo, a lank-haired, blackhead-ridden young man wearing a black cap back to front, is a nice boy and with a nickname like Dodo (meaning sleep in French), has nowhere to go but up in my opinion. Emmanuel has apparently been writing this rock opera for years and it is never quite ready; it always needs a little work. They are all three dressed in black. I, of course unable to help myself where colours are concerned, am dressed in chartreuse and paprika with a pink scarf tying up my hair. In the studio

Gabriel and Dodo grapple with the task of singing and recording a song that neither of them has seen or heard before. The scene is like a Fellini movie, sans the colour, in which conversations aren't making sense but no one is prepared to say that. Emmanuel has not brought the score with him, so he hums the tune to them, changing key every second note.

Gabriel records his keyboard rendition, Dodo orchestrates it via the computer, then Emmanuel (who can't sing) sings the song but the lyrics don't fit the accompaniment. They go over it and over it. I stare through the glass at Gabriel to see if he is as astounded at the preposterousness of the situation as I am. He shows nothing and Dodo is a vision of calm and Zen – totally relaxed, even making positive comments. I am used to action, lights, efficiency. If you ran a restaurant the way you record a song, chefs would die of hunger. This leads me to my next thought – food. I'm hungry. We're all hungry. Gabriel sends Dodo out for food.

'Just get something simple,' he shouts. 'Monbazillac and foie gras will do.'

What a joke. Dodo comes back from the hunt with hamburgers and warm cask wine. Gabriel opens his eyes wide.

'Putain de merde, get a life,' says Dodo, slapping the bags down on the table. 'It's Sunday out there and this isn't Paris, man. This is where real people live. This is south-west France where men are men and we don't eat food with the eyes popping out of it or anything that hasn't been cooked to within an inch of its life.'

He looks at me and winks, unwrapping the hamburgers as if they were mana from heaven and carefully putting them on filthy plates for us. The food is then zapped in a microwave, which appears to be slower than a convection oven.

'Yum,' enthuses Emmanuel, 'these hamburgers are delectable.' The fact that we might get botulism or maybe even paralytic gastroenteritis, not to mention cancer from the burnt bits, is nothing compared with the risks of crossing a road (for example), I think. We open the wine and get drunk immediately on one glass each and exchange information about where we'd rather be. I would like to be listening to opera in a gilt and velvet theatre, but no one else would on the grounds that opera sucks. Dodo and Emmanuel would rather be at a rock concert on the grounds that they could all wear their caps back to front and take drugs. Gabriel says he's happy where he is, thank you, and can we get on with the job.

The recording studio is actually in Dodo's apartment, which closely resembles a World War One bunker – just after a raid and before the rations have arrived. Situated under a factory, it is built to withstand nuclear attack, visitors and the influx of oxygen. An underworld, but at least an underworld you can get out of. It's hot in there and everyone is starting to look like un-wrung dishcloths. The bunker has no windows, no light, no air and the decor is strictly downtown Beirut. I meditate on whether fetid recording studios, in sufficient doses, could be fatal. I can see this is the home of a man who has far better things to occupy his mind than interior decorating and housekeeping. After all, this guy is a magician.

I go for a walk outside and am almost knocked unconscious by fresh air and blinding light. I can't understand people who don't need light in their lives. How can you not be a depressive living in permanent autumn? How could you put on make-up properly? How do you motivate yourself to get out of bed in the morning? The answer is, if you are a musician you don't consider getting up till two and if you are a bass player, for example, a morbid atmosphere would be essential for creativity. Things morbid and dark are a side of life that I'm not particularly attracted to. I wander back into the recording studio and see that things are more relaxed and inhibitions have loosened now that everyone has had a drink. Dodo fiddles around with the guitar adding bits to the soundtrack while Gabriel taps information into the computer. They add and subtract instruments, adjust rhythm, search everywhere for a rap beat, lose it, scream, start again. Emmanuel recommences, making up the violin part as he goes along. Gabriel throws his hands in the air and walks out into the antechamber where I am sitting.

'Merde. I can't fucking stand it!' he says to me, running his hands through his hair. 'I'm going to kill them.'

'What exactly is it you want to do?' I ask him at the risk

of getting my lights punched out. He gazes through the window at the computer.

'I want more of a jazz flow to it. I want someone who can bloody well sing in a straight line. I want something to take it up and out of the ordinary. Christ, I want anything.' He bursts out laughing.

'I can sing,' I say. 'Why don't you get rid of Emmanuel and let me do it?'

He turns to look at me.

'You can sing, Peta?'

'Yes. I can sing.'

He pushes me into the recording room. I put my mouth to the microphone, open it and sing.

'This is great!' Dodo shouts. 'It's wonderful, it's ad lib, it's free expression, more is less, less is more.'

'Génial,' enthuses Emmanuel.

'I want things to be ordered,' I say. 'I want a score. I want the tune written down in front of me so at least I can sight-read.'

Gabriel puts his arms around me. 'Oh yes of course, my chou. You're doing exactly what we want; all we really need now is for you to sing the right tune.'

They write down the words and notes. Gabriel picks up the guitar, Emmanuel hums with me, and it sounds like something is happening.

'Okay, we're going to go for it,' says Gabriel. 'Emmanuel OUT. You're non-essential.'

I am sure I can do it but maybe not the way Emmanuel

wants it done. Dodo is sure it's going to be sensational and Gabriel is sure he's onto something. Anything. He starts the orchestration, gives me the signal to come in, closes his eyes and smiles. With Emmanuel out of the room I simply open my mouth and lovely melodies flow out. The voice warms up, moves around, gets on down to the depths and soars straight through the concrete ceiling into the blue sky. I am in ecstasy. There I was singing in a bunker with a bunch of nutcases. The non-essentials rush into the room, clapping.

'Maintenant, mes enfants,' says Emmanuel. 'The next thing I need is a chorus in this song and guess what? Everyone here is in the chorus, including non-essentials.'

'I can't sing,' says Gabriel.

'I can't sing,' says the incredulous Dodo.

'We can't sing, we've proved it,' say the non-essentials.

Emmanuel remains calm and determined. 'Oh ye of little faith. I can't sing either but that's okay. We'll chant.' He gathers the chanters around me and teaches the lines to a chorus comprising people who have never held a tune in their lives, let alone a microphone. Any cats, preschool children or dogs on heat that might wander in now would be right at home with this lot. The sweating, clogged chorus falls in around the microphone, arms around each another, droning, whispering, croaking and barking their way through the shortest but most stentorian lines of music ever given tongue to. Emmanuel is in heaven. By now it's getting late and I signal to Gabriel that I've had enough bunker synergy and look around in the mess of wires for my bag. There's nothing like music to transform and unite.

• • •

And so the weekend goes. Make love, eat, sing, make love, eat, sing. We eat the truffles with pasta and walnut oil, drink the wine and listen to jazz. This is a testing of the waters. If he fits into my world and I fit into his, we'll be fitting into each other in no time. Gabriel's picture-perfect village, complete with eighth-century abbey, is taken for granted by him and absorbed in fascination by me. Huge keys lock all the doors when we leave reluctantly to drive back to Paris, where I live. We don't want to leave the countryside, but by the time we hit Paris the excitement and energy of the place sweeps us up, entering our blood like a transfusion.

When we arrive at my home on rue de la Grande Chaumière, my flatmate is there and the dining room table full with my chattering, laughing friends in a haze of cigarette smoke. The women are dressed in that inimitable French style where nothing is left to chance, and the men in what Gabriel calls 'rich-casual' – jeans, silk scarves and linen jackets. There's a gesture to food in the form of bits of cheese on the table, but I can see the real nourishment is the wine and cigarettes. The music of Nino Rota is playing. Gabriel stays the night then drives back down to the Dordogne, leaving me feeling like a swollen honey bee, full of the joys of living, positively poisoned with love, seeing la vie en rose. I know he feels the same way. I think about him and mentally follow his car all the way down to the Dordogne – tunnelling a corridor of electric cobalt light into him. If we weren't able to use this transforming energy of love, food and music in our lives, where would we be?

My Brush with Mental Illness

Drugs are vehicles for people who have forgotten how to walk.

The Anatomy of Restlessness *by Bruce Chatwin*

Me: Hi, I'm Peta. I'm doing staff training. I'm not an addict but I'm working on it. What are you in for?

Dope Fiend: I'm here because I gave my baby downers to make it sleep and it didn't wake up. I'm a slimy drug addict. I hate myself more than I do the whole world and I've tried to commit suicide five times.

Me: Oh . . . right.

Dope Fiend: So when are you going to stop kidding yourself and everyone else that you have no problems and why are you making jokes about it?

Me: I beg your pardon?

Dope Fiend: (shouting) I said why are you fucking smiling, arsehole?!

Me: Cripes. Because I'm a naturally happy person and I make jokes to help people be happy too.

Dope Fiend: What bullshit. I could vomit. What filth went on in your childhood that you have to make jokes all the time? What are you covering up?

Me: Nothing that a few needles wouldn't have cured except that I had a thing called 'strength of character'. Okay, so my mother slept with my father but I got over it.

Dope Fiend: (screaming) You spoiled, middle-class, overfed WASP . . .

Me: (screaming to get into the rhythm) Catholic! New Zealander! Catholic!

Dope Fiend: (screaming but now with more respect – they were mostly from religious if not Catholic families) You're not getting out of this toilet till you wipe that smile off your face and share with me the wounded inner child who had to be funny. Why do you have to be liked so much? Why can't you have a serious conversation about real emotions?

Me: (upset and shocked) Because I don't know you and I'm not sick and I'm just here for training and it's none of your business.

Dope Fiend: (screaming, practically frothing) What do I have to do to get you to take a look at yourself? I can see from a hundred paces that you're covering something up. Why can't you be serious?

Me: (weeping) Because if I don't laugh I'll cry. Because I can't stand the tension. Because no one liked me till I invented my present personality. The first personality didn't work.

Dope Fiend: Well I'm not too enthralled with the present one. Go and scrub the dining room floor again.

All I knew about residential drug treatment when I arrived at the centre where this conversation took place was what I had gleaned from the brochure and my job interview. I walked into my new counselling job with a trusting smile, a misplaced missionary complex and a recipe for good living. I really believed in the power of transformation. The graceful lodge, surrounded by a moat and stunningly ordered grounds divided up by paths like a Monopoly set, was hidden away at the back of the town. The entrance into this world was my introduction to emotional toxicity, Lady-Macbeth-style compulsiveness and gaping broken hearts. This was a world of dope fiends and alcoholics; young people so damaged you wondered how they were still walking around. The residential treatment centre, called Portage, engaged in the deconstruction and reconstruction of personalities. The brochure said the therapy was to help residents achieve personal growth and free themselves from addiction.

I wasn't addicted to anything myself but that was just a fluke – it wasn't strength of character because I had tried everything. It just appeared that one of my few gifts was a lack of addiction. Once I have had enough champagne, coke, caviar, trick pelvises, mink coats, whatever, I just stop. However, I am extremely attracted to negativity, and if you have had a childhood full of wicked stepmothers eating their children, Jesus being flogged and wholesale saint rape, the chances of you being a little flower in a field are slim. Next to the people at Portage the rampaging Sisters of Mercy from my tender years were just underachievers; the matrons of my training hospital simpering pretenders; the mother a walk in the park. The word portage or portaging refers to the practice of carrying watercraft or cargo over land to avoid river obstacles, or between two bodies of water. A place where this carrying occurs is also called a portage. Sounds lovely. Looked lovely when you visited – beautiful, disturbingly clean and ordered, dope fiends going about their daily tasks. Parents were always impressed to see their previously degraded children cleaning their teeth and looking normal. It wasn't till you moved in that you realised how little your life skills of apple crumble making and guitar playing were going to count. Well . . . not *exactly* because it turned out I was the best cook they had ever had and trying to pass myself off as Joni Mitchell was highly appreciated.

Many therapists had tried to work at Portage and failed after a few weeks due to lack of backbone – to being morally flaccid. After I left, dope fiends told me they would have gladly crawled back to prison on their bellies and eaten cockroach soufflés had they genuinely felt they had the choice. The fiends were encouraged to call themselves 'the family' – just like Charles Manson. The first part of my training involved spending one month in treatment, living with the fiends as if I were one, sleeping with them, eating with them and being treated like them. If I survived that, I would then be put on staff and my training would continue in a more formal way. This is how the routine went: up at 7 a.m. and to bed at midnight if you were lucky. In between you worked, cleaned, cooked, gardened, talked non-stop about how sick you were (you weren't allowed to stop talking for one second – some people just repeated the same thing over and over again), received therapy, yelled and got yelled at. The idea was to not have any mental, physical or emotional safe havens – dope fiends had to be confronted unremittingly, to the point where it became an empty performance, a loud routine where you bawled at people instead of talking to them.

'How are you going there?'

'I'm tired. I fell asleep with my head on the toilet bowl and now I have a contusion.'

'You're tired? What have you ever done in your life that would make you tired? I'm asking you about your feelings.'

'Feelings?'

'YEAH, FEELINGS!'

This was followed by a bulb-shattering diatribe. You may be surprised to learn that the treatment was based on army practices. Dope fiends were so desperate to get away from the warm embrace of their betters at Portage that sometimes they hid in the house. One kid climbed into the ceiling of the dormitory and fell asleep. The entire house was placed on deserter alert, we drag-netted that building like an ant colony on a tedious outing. I personally was hoping the kid was in a tree somewhere sticking needles up his wazoo. Eventually he was discovered when he fell through the ceiling onto the plant display, unconscious.

The concept of evil and the devil began to fascinate me. In my nightmares in that first month at Portage, I regressed straight back to childhood. Along with the guilt nightmares, the being late nightmares and the matricidal nightmares, came the evil nightmares. You will go to the devil, to hell, you are born in a state of putrid sin and only true conversion and purity will save you from roasting forever. In Catholicism you don't just roast, you roast for eternity day after day after day. Nightly I woke up shaking with palpitating heart and drenched body. I had no language or training to connect my inner life with the stuff I listened to all day in my outer life at Portage. My secular imagination was reaching for old religious metaphors to cope. At the same time as I was repelled by both the addicts and the methods of the therapists, I found the drama and negativity and the possibility that I could actually bring some light into these people's lives (at best) and teach the girls not to wear pink and red in the same outfit (at least) alluring. If I couldn't participate in the transformation story, why was I there?

I never slept more than a few hours a night because of the nightmares, the snoring of other inmates (we slept in bunks in shared rooms) and the strangeness of my surroundings. Pleading exhaustion was greeted with derision and the information that tiredness brought with it a breaking down of resistance. The more tired you are, the less you lie. The pressure never stopped, you were confronted at every turn; nothing was as it appeared. The aggression was unthinkable for an ordinary person because nobody behaves like that in real life except when they are genuinely angry. Even though I had had an emotionally colourful childhood, I had nevertheless been brought up to not make a fuss *too* often, never to be angry towards authority and to have a modicum of respect for other people. Lying on my bunk in teeshirt and jeans and no make-up I thought, *I can't do this.* I'm just going to wash the director's feet with my tears, dry them with my hair, apologise for being superficial and attention-seeking and leave. When I announced this in the little wooden office with check curtains, the director of treatment said, 'No, no. You must stay. You're doing very well. We believe you've got what it takes.'

As it turned out I was acquainted with one of the residents – a charismatic chap named Philippe. The staff knew we were acquainted so we were mostly kept apart. On the surface he seemed to be mirroring his life on the outside. He was popular, hard-working, funny, got caught having sex with a girl in the toilets (sex and relationships were forbidden) and was progressing fast up the hierarchy ladder at Portage. I wasn't taken in by it but he was so much more educated and socially sophisticated than most of the other wretched sinners, that it didn't take much for him to become a natural leader. It appeared most of the staff were charmed by him also. Once, I did corner him outside doing some gardening.

'How are you doing, Philippe?' I asked, squatting down and weeding beside him.

'It's too easy for me to play the game.'

'Do you want to stop using?'

'When I decide to, Peta, I'll just stop. Weeping because my father slapped me is not going to touch any deep rivers in me.'

I smiled. 'Don't get too smart with yourself, honey – there's nothing the peasants like more than to see the king in his new clothes.'

'Life is so boring without drugs. Ordinary life is not enough any more.'

'Oh Philippe, what about the sunset and the sparkling icicle trees and the taste of freshly roasted chestnuts?'

'Don't notice sunsets or trees and can't taste food any more. It's all too subtle and banal. Once you've lived on speed and coke you can never settle for real life again – it's too hackneyed and trite.'

'You must try harder,' I pleaded. I couldn't bear to lose Philippe. If he wasn't cured then my recipe for living had failed. To me, he had so many admirable qualities but he didn't perceive himself as having a problem. It's like the chicken crossing the road. He never wanted to get to the other side; he was happy where he was. It was the person helping the chicken who wanted it to get to the other side of the road.

I didn't want to be dragged under by this strange hidden world at Portage myself, but in the end only just got out in time. Philippe and Louise were the reasons I stayed so long. Like Philippe, Louise was far too intelligent and sane to be involved in such an outfit. She was a very competent psychologist who had the tools and solid professional understanding to monitor the group therapy sessions, but the thing that worried me about Portage was that no one else on the staff came anywhere near her ability or training and they were dealing with severely disintegrated personalities. Most of the therapists were recovered addicts themselves, bolstered up by a few staff like me with medical or social-work backgrounds. As the months went by I saw under-skilled therapists push borderline psychotics into bottomless hells from which they risked never returning. Sometimes clients sank fast, which is easy to do once you've been given permission. Several times Louise had to be called in to save the day before someone defenestrated.

At the end of a month in residence I was deemed suitable, tough enough material to go on staff training for three months, and I moved into Louise's cottage on the property – a pretty, comfortable little house full of books, plants and antiques. Snow covered everything outside like a meringue. Frozen rain would fall, followed by a sudden drop in temperature – the result of which was soft snow underfoot with a crisp layer of ice on top – deliciously crunchy to walk on and very dangerous. The trees were giant icicles and the atmosphere pale blue and misty like a dream. Portage was a very beautiful old building and, okay, so there were good times like the dances where everyone got dressed up to kill or at least maim, like the special festive dinners, and Louise's sex education classes were even more startling than mine had ever been. The dope fiends, in spite of their precocious sexual experience, didn't know anything about the hydraulics of sex. Most people don't, as it turns out.

Why did I stay? I'd determined that I would come hell or high water, just as a personal challenge. It was my there's-got-to-be-more-to-life-than-shopping-and-gin stage. Maybe there is and maybe there isn't, but if you can do shopping and gin with joy, you're way ahead of most people. I chose the long way round to find that out. Most people used drugs to get into Portage. It was drugs that got me out. The majority of the residents were young men from poorly educated, unskilled backgrounds, whose fathers, brothers, uncles or priests had sometimes sexually abused them. A lot of the girls had had sexual relationships with their brothers and male relatives. This was the first time I had seen the damage done by incest and the related movement to anaesthetising drug-taking. All the skeletons came out of the closet and the chickens came home to roost in droves.

My flatmates Bonny and Shelley in Montreal and I called each other regularly so I could maintain a grip on reality, and we talked about our love lives. One was dating the boy across the road and the other was dating his flatmate. I, needless to say, was dating nobody in my drug Armageddon. In spite of my stable personality, I was finding the influence of the Portage lifestyle was resulting in what I can only describe as my losing touch or floating. Even the way I talked had changed and become robot-like. It was only when I was in Montreal on a break that my friends, and even I, noticed how vague I was. It was great to be back in their normal world, but I was firm in my resolve not to capitulate and to go as far as I could go at Portage. I had learned that, after negotiating city traffic, intimate relationships were the leading cause of anger in the world. Up until Portage I had always found the most productive and mature way to express anger was to pull the curtains down and throw them into oncoming traffic or something. With therapy I now felt I knew better and informed my friends that I was a changed woman.

'You sound terrible, Peta,' Bonny fretted. 'You are speaking so slowly and you sound so reasonable. Are you drugged or something?'

'No. I'm getting in touch with my primal inner bitch and becoming whole.'

'Christ.'

'And I'm sorry I called all those men pig-dog-male-ego-testicle-imperialists.'

'Peta, I'm coming down there right now to get you. This has gone far enough. You've been brain-washed. We love you because you're exciting and unpredictable and mouthy . . .'

'Unpredictable is just another word for mad.'

'You're not mad.'

'Don't lie.'

'Okay, you're still normal. I won't get on the next train but I'm still worried. Make sure you stay in touch. If anything happens in that strange place you call us, you hear – any time of the day or night.'

Winter turned to summer in a day. There didn't seem to be a spring or an autumn in this Canadian land of extremes. Quebec has as extreme a summer as it has a winter with endless blue, flower-infested, thirty-five-degree days. Summer at Portage was an explosion of spectacular colour – picturesque cottages, wild flowers and berries on the sides of the narrow roads, old wooden churches, weeping willows, buzzing bugs and molten, ardent heat. There was also a lot of molten, ardent stuff going on in 'hostility' groups and one-on-one therapy indoors at the centre. I had settled into the abuse that was called therapy with frightening ease, but it was slowly dawning on me that what I was doing wasn't actually working. I had been there a year when I started to notice that, once they graduated from the centre and left, some of the cured dope fiends became big drinkers. It didn't happen in a start of realisation – it happened gradually that I understood how deeply I didn't fit in, how unappreciated my apple crumble was, how resented my Scarlett O'Hara straw sun-hats were, what a flawed role model I was in the get-a-life department. But these props allowed me to pretend that I was somehow different from my charges.

One sunny day, without any warning, I was summonsed to a special confrontation group. I was in a good mood and wearing my sun-hat. When I walked in I saw the group comprised only staff, from the most junior to the most senior, about eight of the toughest people in the universe – my colleagues and friends. A chill breeze blew across the ravines of my soul. I sat quietly in the chair, hardened my resolve with good posture, put my hands in my lap and felt as a male praying mantis would feel when he realised that the pleasure of sex was going to be interrupted by his inamorata sinking her jaws into his head. My mind was rapidly scanning my work at Portage for a therapeutic mistake I had made, a joke that had backfired, some sleazy dope fiend I had maybe exchanged bodily fluids with without noticing. But this confrontation was for me. The interrogation was about my using hard drugs with an inmate. It was so fatuous that I laughed in their faces, which resulted in a circle of piercing cries of contempt. This went on for hours and hours into the night, sans food or sleep. I can see why prisoners admit to betraying their country when interrogated. I would have said I put razor blades in my eyes and gave myself ecstasy enemas, I was so exhausted. Like barking dogs, they were hell-determined to make me confess to something – anything – but it's surprisingly difficult to remember putting cocaine up your nose when you haven't. I even got out twenty-dollar notes to show them how clean they were.

Where did it come from? Why had they turned against their 'star' therapist? Portage was a very wound-up, closed community and one suspicious whisper was all it took. In that place of suppurating wounds, terrible things *did* happen that shouldn't have happened – like the time a boy slit his wrists and the time a girl got heroin into the house. Even Philippe having sex in the toilets was unthinkable in that setting. The staff resented my friendship with the erudite Louise and considered me a bit of a snob. The basis of most deceptions is seeded in mistrust and jealousy and I suspected their readiness to believe the worst of me was based in this most ordinary and old-fashioned of emotions. My protestations and clean bank notes were eventually enough to satisfy their blood lust, but only temporarily. The next day it was announced that I had to nevertheless confess my behaviour to the whole enthralled family, apologise to them and go back into treatment. By then I had had some sleep and got my mojo back. At this point I began to feel vaguely threatened and called the girls in Montreal.

I couldn't morally indulge the therapists in this confession pantomime, no matter how titivating it would be for the family and didn't feel I had the right dress to wear for such an occasion, so resigned on the spot. Louise, my shape-shifting friend, had joined the tormentors and turned me into a war criminal. But, in the fetid atmosphere of Portage, by evening and in the face of my righteous anger, they had backed down and begged me to stay, realising they had gone too far. But it was too late. I had had the life squeezed out of me, been under-paid and now betrayed – they had believed an addict over me. I felt I was in some sort of danger but didn't know what. I felt they were looking for a big humiliation scene – like a country hopes for a war to motivate restless youth. Bonny said, 'Trust your instincts. If you don't feel safe, you're not safe. I think you should make a move sooner rather than later.' In the dark of night she and Shelley drove two hours from Montreal into the Portage complex and I quietly walked out, leaving behind a bunch of low-life criminals – and that was just the staff. The one last thing I did of worth before I left was to apologise to all the dope fiends I had screamed at and leave them my apple crumble recipe.

The moral of this story is similar to the joke, 'How many therapists does it take to change a light bulb? Only one, but the light bulb has to really want to change.' People who don't want to change won't change, no matter how much help they get, and there is no scientific proof whatsoever that screaming is good for your mental health. My experience at Portage was the primary dinner-party story among my friends and colleagues for years after. The story would usually start with something like: 'Do you remember the time you lost your mind, Peta?' or 'Have you found a lawyer to lay charges against those people yet, Peta?' or 'Tell the people how you got cured of your missionary complex and released your inner Nazi, Peta' or 'Peta, can you do your toilet-cleaning demonstration?' With this party trick, we handed out ear plugs.

So much for transformation.

Channelling Edith

Qu'on soit riche ou sans un sous
Sans amour on n'est rien du tout.
(It doesn't matter whether you're rich
or poor,
Without love you're nothing.)

From 'La Goualante Du Pauvre Jean'
Edith Piaf

In 1915, six days before Christmas, a poverty-stricken teenage cabaret singer named Line Marsa gave birth to a tiny baby girl whom she called Edith Giovanna Gassion. Father Louis was off drunk in a bar, so she had to deliver Edith on her own. Myth has it the baby was born right on the pavement outside 72 rue de Belleville in Paris, but in reality she was probably born at Tenon Hospital. She wasn't well looked after, both parents were drunks, and as a child Edith lived her life as best she could on the streets.

When she was a teenager she had a daughter of her own who died as a baby of neglect and illness. Louis Gassion was a street acrobat and took Edith everywhere with him. How could anyone know that this malnourished little kid would turn out to be one of the greatest singers in history? She was to become Edith Piaf.

I was a teenager myself the first time I heard Piaf's voice. A school boyfriend had come back from a trip to Tahiti with an extremely unusual record. The woman sang in an old-fashioned voice full of drama and despair. The orchestration was, to my ears, unfamiliar and seemed overwrought. At that time we were all listening to The Beatles and Donovan. My friend and I were both French students and he persisted in playing this record to me over and over again while explaining what the singer was saying and enthusing about how magical it was. Gradually, I too came to love it. My friends thought I was very eccentric for listening to this music, which they didn't understand. But then I was also studying opera and loved country and folk singing, so eccentric was the neutral gear of my musical taste. I realised years later that what all these seemingly disparate musical styles had in common was their sad storylines. To me, opera was country music with classy arias. Piaf's singing was rooted in music hall, which I knew nothing about, but I liked the plaintive accordion accompaniment. As a teenager, I didn't yet know what deception and heartbreak meant, so there was something forbidden, sordid and worldly about these Piaf songs. Listening to that record marked the beginning of my lifelong interest in poignant songs. Many years later I decided to write a book about Piaf and the tradition of sad singing in other cultures over the world. I haven't written that book yet, but I got quite far in my Piaf research.

• • •

There is a sad song tradition in Greece called rembetika. Rembetika music was originally an underground tradition that started in the lower-class hash houses of Piraeus and Thessaloniki at the turn of last century, with the forced immigration of two million Greek refugees from Asia Minor. It is the beautiful, sad singing of the displaced, with their shattered dreams and sense of betrayal. The lyrics were often written in coded language for fear of persecution. The songs are accompanied by a bouzouki and saz (like a lute) with a strong oriental influence in the rhythm. In Ireland, the sad songs are the sean-nós. They are an early seventeenth-century tradition of unaccompanied songs, probably originating from French Provençal troubadour songs of the thirteenth and fourteenth centuries. Most of what is still sung today originated in the eighteenth century and they are generally laments and sad love stories – an ancient form of journalism wherein people were informed of the news in other parts – and formal, extremely poetic and long 'big songs'. Sean-nós are very ornamented, and to listen to this fusion of poetry and music is like hearing melodies grow out of words as if flowers were oozing honey right in front of you. The rhythm and style is profoundly embedded in the ancient Gaelic language and poetry, and is effectively untranslatable because the language is used so differently. There are also traditional dances that go with rembetika and sean-nós. Of course, there are many more sad song traditions, such as American country music, Japanese enka, Māori waiata, Portuguese fado, Spanish laments and so on . . .

● ● ●

The first thing I discovered on my sentimental 'channelling Edith' trip to Paris was the Place Edith Piaf in the working-class 20th arrondissement. The day after I arrived, I walked out the door of my friend's house on rue Saint-Fargeau and aimlessly strolled in the sunshine till something happened. A good way to get things done, I find. I had forgotten that Piaf was born in the 20th, and within minutes there I was sipping an espresso at the Bar de la Place Edith Piaf. This ordinary little neighbourhood bar sits opposite the entrance to the Porte de Bagnolet Métro. All over the walls are Piaf's photos, together with a poster of a poem dedicated to her. She's even etched on the window. There were Edith-embossed souvenirs for sale, so I bought a lighter to keep in my bag because one's French friends are always running out of matches to light their Gauloises, n'est-ce pas? There was a bottle of Bourgogne déclassé with a photo of Edith on the label that tempted me, but I resisted. The bar menu on the blackboard had pâté de l'Aveyron, and I thought fondly of my French sister-in-law Aline, who is from the Aveyron Valley, a gastronomic nirvana in the south-west of France. She always lilts, 'Tout est bon en Aveyron.' Everything is good in Aveyron.

I continued on my way in search of a market to buy my lunch, and to this end stopped two elderly ladies and asked directions. A huge conversation ensued as to the nearest market, their ability or not to walk to it, and the relative values of their ages.

'Bien sûr que Madame peut marcher jusqu'au marché. Vous êtes une jeune femme, voyons.' Of course the lady can walk to the market – you're a young woman. She pointed down the road.

'Et toi, tu peux marcher jusque là?' she asked her elderly friend. And can you walk that far?

'Bien sûr que non. Je fais quoi pour toi?' Of course I can't. How old do you think I am?

In the time-honoured tradition of people who wish to maintain their friendships, the other woman underestimated her friend's age. 'Quatre-vingt cinq.' Eighty-five.

But not by much.

'Eh bien, j'ai quatre-vingt sept.' Well, I'm eighty-seven!

'Comment? Moi, j'ai soixante-dix-huit et je marche toujours facilement jusqu'au marché.' What? I'm seventy-eight and I can still walk easily to the market.

'Tu vois, ces neuf ans font toute la différence.' You see, those nine years make all the difference.

The 20th arrondissement is still working-class and full of faubourgs – suburbs – with bars and cafés, the Bois de Vincennes and the Canal Saint-Martin. I put my head in at the Java dance hall on the rue du Faubourg du Temple. The last time I was there, in the 1990s, dark gentlemen in white suits and ladies d'un certain âge dressed up like cocottes, danced the waltz, the tango, the rumba and the paso doblé. The place reeked of pastis and nostalgia – I was enchanted. Piaf used to sing there – songs like 'Bal Dans Ma Rue' were inspired by it; songs about street dancing, drinking and lovers. Now the Java offers pop rock and electro break, but it is still different from any other club in Paris – very friendly and unpretentious. I wanted to hear a contemporary singer channelling Piaf, so I called in on a bar on rue de la Gaieté in Montparnasse, which was well known for its singing. The patron told me he normally had a woman singing Piaf songs but she was on holiday, and as he couldn't stand Piaf he was very happy about her absence.

• • •

The 20th arrondissement is now rather funky, especially the Quartier Saint-Blaise. Slightly secretive, it is quiet, harmonious, clean and spacious – an artistic quarter full of painters, sculptors and teaching ateliers. There are lots of very atmospheric restaurants, bars and cafés, and of course, the desperately hip Mama Shelter hotel. Even though Mama Shelter is a long way from my favourite shopping haunts, I now always stay there because I love the atmosphere in the hotel and I feel that the 20th arrondissement is a very real and honest part of Paris that most visitors never see. Mama Shelter has comfortable stylish rooms, a good restaurant under the direction of Alain Ducasse, and decor by Philippe Starck. Its inhabitants range from rock stars to families to designers to artists. The plat du jour and nightly entertainment is written in white ink on the mirrors in the foyer on each floor. Every night rocks at Mama – Edith would have loved it because she could have drunk there all night. Across the road is the famous Flèche d'Or, a big seedy bar overlooking the railway lines. It is like something out of *Pulp Fiction* and has huge motorbikes parked outside, screaming chefs and grindingly filthy decor. A popular joint for rock concerts, it has revolting unisex toilets. Men are already lucky that we talk to them – now we have to share the toilet with them? Walking up the road to the Porte de Bagnolet Métro, you find the Edith Piaf café, and if you walk a bit the other way you find the Père Lachaise cemetery, where Edith sleeps under a simple polished granite slab in the north-east corner. It is still topped with bunches and bunches of fresh roses, because after all and in spite of everything, she always saw la vie en rose.

• • •

In 2001 a publisher friend gave me the phone number of an elderly journalist who had been one of Piaf's friends. I called and made an appointment to see her. Sylvaine Pecheral was in her seventies and opened her door in the salubrious 16th arrondissement with the greeting, 'Yes hello, what is it you want exactly and what did you say your name was?' I gulped like a fish out of water and was ushered into a small flat that immediately reminded me of an artist's digs. A real Ali Baba's cave, this place was filled from top to bottom, every wall, every table, every shelf, with stuff. A compulsive collector, Sylvaine had literally thousands of miniature antique dolls, toys, houses, music boxes, musical instruments, trains, cars, bears, soldiers and puppets. She had a huge library of books on cinema and entertainment and stacks of 45s and LPs. There were photos of her as a young woman all over the place – long blonde hair in voluptuous curls, an intelligent, beautiful face and the look of a movie star. The woman sitting opposite me, dressed in a black teeshirt and black pants, still had long, thick, healthy blonde hair tied at the base of the neck with a black velvet ribbon. Her skin was creamy and the beauty she once had was still visible, if faded – large brown eyes full of mischief, pink lipstick, perfect make-up.

It became obvious quite quickly that Sylvaine wanted to talk about herself more than she did Piaf, which was okay with me. I had done enough research on Piaf to fill the Pompidou Centre. Sylvaine had written for all the big magazines and newspapers, presented a jazz radio show, interviewed everyone who was anyone on both radio and television, and had the photos to prove it. She showed me albums full of her with them – Josephine Baker, Fernandel, Ingrid Bergman, Brassens, Yves Montand (who was her lover for a time), Marilyn Monroe, Picasso, Piaf, Cerdan, Pagnol, Jean Marais. *Everyone.* As the interview progressed, the wine came out and we spent the afternoon laughing, drinking, discussing all the gossip about who was gay, who slept with whom, who Sylvaine had slept with, who wanted to marry her, who she regretted not marrying. She married a gay man and stayed with him for a year, lived with various others but never married again and didn't have children. She'd lived in this same flat since 1943.

• • •

Channelling Edith, I left Paris and headed south. In Marseille I came across people dancing the tango in a square in the hot night, but they weren't singing Piaf. In Roquefort-les-Pins, though, I was served a pleasant surprise. My friends were playing Piaf interpreted by various French singers – Johnny Hallyday, Serge Gainsbourg and Charles Aznavour. Aznavour was a very close friend of Piaf and in 1997 recorded a new version of her classic 'Plus Bleu Que Tes Yeux'. Using modern technology, studio technicians were able to resurrect Piaf's voice from old recordings and mix it with Aznavour's vocals, producing a stunning virtual duet. We sat around the pool sipping pastis, listening to these heavenly love songs full of betrayal, deception and disappointment. I was delighted, for this was exactly what I wanted. Roquefort-les-Pins is in the mountains above Nice, and the house my friends were staying in for the August holidays was on a large property graced with forest walks, a swimming pool and a large terrace. The house belonged to a world-famous art dealer in Paris, and the pale stone walls of the interior of the refurbished farmhouse were covered with the paintings of Luis Lemos. Everywhere were violent clashes of colour, voluptuous portrayals of the human body, fantastic studies in light. Even the walls of the laundry and caretaker's cottage out the back had large erotic art works on them. Each night, before going to bed, I went out onto the balcony off my room and watched the lights of Nice tango with the stars.

One warm August evening, sitting around the table after a grand aioli, I sang my favourite Piaf song 'Hymne à l'Amour' – 'If You Love Me' – written by Piaf and put to music by Marguerite Monnot. It is a love song that encapsulates for me how Piaf was in her own life: it talks of reckless passion, excessive declarations of fidelity and is full of a sort of morose self-pity which conveys the idea that if all else fails, at least the lovers will be happy in heaven if not in this miserable valley of tears. Edith describes what she would do for her man – go to the ends of the earth, unhook the moon, steal a fortune, betray her country, betray her friends and even dye her hair blonde. This kind of raw sentiment is right up my alley. Marguerite Monnot was a very beautiful composer with blonde hair, big blue eyes, creamy skin and pink lips – the opposite of Edith, who was dark-haired and Gallic-looking with hooded eyes. Edith's first and most important impresario, Raymond Asso, had persuaded her to work with Monnot. Different as they were, they became best friends. Edith was only twenty-four when she wrote the words to this song, but she had had many lovers since the age of fifteen and had the street experience of a much older woman. When Asso picked her up she was twenty, practically illiterate and didn't even know which knives and forks to use at the table. He taught her how to dress, how to talk clearly and what to do with herself on stage (she always said the reason her hands were crossed over her heart when she sang was because she didn't know what else to do with them). Asso was responsible for a lot of Edith's success – she repaid him by treating him very badly then dumping him.

Piaf, who often didn't use a microphone on stage, had a voice like a powerful wind – she could whisper 'je t'aime' to a room of two thousand people. Everyone felt she was whispering to them alone. She used to say, 'A song is a story but the audience must be able to believe in it. I'm the lover, my song must be sad, it must be a cry from the heart, it's my life. The words must be simple, my audience shouldn't have to think but in their bellies they should respond to my voice. There should be poetry too, the kind to make them dream.' This is the true magic of her songs. Even when you sing them to people who don't understand French, there is always an emotional reaction. People really do respond to the voice with their bellies. This is where sad songs or indeed songs of betrayal and love in any culture are similar. You could sing a traditional Irish ballad of deception and lost love to French friends and they would be desperate with sadness mixed with the pleasure of a beautiful tune.

• • •

Saying au revoir to my friends, I left Rochefort-les-Pins to go on to the most dazzling town on the Riviera, Cannes, where I knew no one and believed I would write as there is nothing else to do, unless you're a film star. Piaf had a villa in the nearby village of Plascassier. It wasn't film-festival time, Hollywood hadn't called, so I rented an apartment in the Suquet in old Cannes to be close to Edith. Cannes is commercial, touristy and festival-oriented now, but it is still in a beautiful setting on La Napoule Bay with a stunning climate, through both winter and summer. Before it was discovered by the English aristocracy in the mid-1800s, it was just an old fishing village on a hill with a particularly beautiful port. It took its name from the reeds (cannas) that grew everywhere. In those days, the ice-cream-cake-like Hotel Splendid hadn't yet been built; the famous Croisette or promenade lined with palm trees and gardens didn't yet exist and neither did the casino, the conference centre or the glamorous rue d'Antibes, full of designer shops. But in old Cannes people still hang their washing from lines outside their windows like flags in the wind, a habit forbidden in Paris. The heat never stops day after day; even when cloudy, my fan with its blades decorated in black lace and bullfighters was in constant use, to the amusement of the natives. In the south of France they just put up with the heat and move slowly.

They eat olives and drink olive oil like there's no tomorrow on the Riviera, and olives are always served with your drink in the upmarket cafés. At a tiny café called Lucullus on the edge of the Forville market in my quarter, I was offered amuse-gueules like eggplant and courgette fritters, tapenade or smashed sardines on toast and sweet tomato concassée. Meridionals start drinking early in the day. At 10 a.m. they're already throwing down the panachés (shandy), kirs (cassis and white wine), pressions (draught beer), rosé, and some form of aniseed – pastis, Pernod, et cetera. In the morning, I swished through the market snapping up olives, berries, tiny aubergines and red peppers, muscat grapes and courgettes that were round like green tennis balls. So, there I was on the very desirable Riviera and for two days I turned in circles and nothing happened. This was in the dark days of 2001, when electronic communication was unimaginably primitive. I discovered that my internet cable, autrement dit my umbilical cord, had been left at Rochefort-les-Pins. There turned out to be no telephone line in the apartment, no oven and no washing machine.

I hadn't met anyone interesting, I was getting nowhere with my Edith research and had writer's block. Two days of not being able to write, talk or email and I was weeping into my soup. Why was I here? Why had I done this? Why wasn't life a party any more? And why was I depressed in one of the most beautiful seaside towns in the world? You mention Cannes or Monte Carlo or Menton up the road to anyone outside France, and they faint with envy imagining casinos on the beach and half-naked starlets more beautiful than the mind can bear without going into synapse overload. No.

Time passed. Slowly and quickly at the same time – the way it does when you have writer's block. On the third day I was already bored with being depressed – so sick of it I could have screamed. Controlling your universe is a wonderful thing, so I sat up straight, smoked a cigarette, had a gin and thought *What would Edith do?* Probably be proactive. Well, kind of. She would have gone out to clubs all night, dragged some young man home, slept till 2 p.m., had a few drinks, downed a few pills then started rehearsing and learning new songs. That third day the sheer force of channelling Edith's energy produced:

- a library full of Piaf and Jacques Brel books
- a new internet cord
- a kind, handsome man called Jean-Pascal at Telecom who not only let me use his personal line for my emails but introduced me to his friends
- a cheap, good restaurant
- a fabulous dress with my name on it from rue d'Antibes on sale.

All in one day. Now I was inspired and unblocked. Okay, so I would have to diet my way into the dress of black and green stretch lace, but so what? It was too hot to eat anyway. My voluptuous bits were draining off by the hour, and I was still doing daily fast walks, which even at nine in the morning were killing in the heat. Here was my typical day in Cannes: up at 9 a.m.; access emails; flirt with Jean-Pascal; fast walk; coffee at market and maybe shopping; write at apartment or research Edith at the library; in the afternoon, down to the beach for a swim; more writing; evening, more writing, reading or out to dinner with new acquaintances. Accessing my emails at Telecom became more and more of a pleasure thanks to Jean-Pascal. If I hadn't had email problems I would have invented them just to see his beautiful brown eyes. Every morning he greeted me as if he had been waiting all his life to see me, insisted I use his office, made me coffee and acted as if his day was ruined when I had to leave. Although he was from central France, to me he looked very Mediterranean with his tanned skin, easy-going nature matched with a certain restlessness and southern sense of humour. About thirty-five, short dark hair, slim, sexy in his fitting jeans and open-necked shirts. He introduced me to all the staff and told them to look out for me. We talked, flirted, he confided in me, I gave lots of free advice about women – we just enjoyed each other's company.

• • •

But back to Edith. In 1934 Louis Maitrier was looking for a young singer for a Radio Vitus orchestra. At the Palais Berlitz in Paris he heard a tiny teenager singing. She was wearing a second-hand black dress and no jewellery, save for the little cross around her neck. She sang like a nightingale in such a simple, touching way that he said to his wife, 'Don't look any more – our singer is here.' I have heard a recording of Piaf singing for that radio show and her voice was very young – high, clear and very much in the forties style, quite unlike the deep husky voice it became after years of abuse – alcohol and smoking. But even at a young age she had an astoundingly powerful, sonorous voice that was deeply moving and had perfect diction. Hers was like a jazz voice, although she had never heard jazz in her life. She was a very bright and determined person, eventually teaching herself to read music, learn English and speak properly in French, thus losing her vulgar Parisian street twang. She was able to record an LP in one sitting and could remember the tune and words of a song having only heard it once. Subsequently, whatever country she performed in, she always learned some of her songs in that language. I've heard recordings of her singing in English and German, and they're wonderful.

I got out my Piaf song books and read the words closely. Songs of betrayal speak not only of personal deceptions but also of political and national tragedies. Piaf's career was already in full swing during the Occupation of France, and like a lot of well-known entertainers, she performed for the troops, visited prisoners of war in Germany and sang ceaselessly at clubs and music halls all over France. One of her most famous songs, 'Non, Je Ne Regrette Rien' – 'No Regrets' – was even taken up by the right-wing Pied Noir Secret Army in Algeria. The music to this defiant song was written by Charles Dumont, who enjoyed a long professional and amorous collaboration with Piaf. In it she sings that she doesn't regret a thing in her life – not the good people have done her, nor the harm. It is all swept away and forgotten because today she starts again with a new man (who is *the* one, needless to say).

This was *the* recurring theme in her work. It didn't matter how much she suffered, how many problems she had with men, tomorrow was always another day, the next man was always going to be the true love of her life. When she met someone she liked, she forgot everyone else. And she never, ever learned from her mistakes. Piaf always said, 'I don't want to be careful with my loves, my life or my money: I'm not a bloody housewife. You don't know what it's like to never have had anything and then to have full pockets and be able to give to others.' Although she was neither beautiful nor shapely, Edith had a magnetic, charismatic personality and even the youngest, most handsome men couldn't resist her. The fact that she was swaggeringly generous probably also helped. She was very matter-of-fact about sex and direct when she wanted a man in her big mauve bed – just got down to business immediately. She didn't make love like a housewife, either. Her sexual voracity was legendary and such was her need for instant gratification that she would pick men up anywhere – on the Métro, in bars, on the street, at performances. She liked big men, especially ones with blue eyes, and had a penchant for sailors, crooks and legionnaires – she loved a uniform. What particularly excited Piaf was playing three men along at once without any of them knowing.

There were many other singers in Piaf's era who sang in a similar style, but they all fell away to her brilliance. To this day no one can remember them – but the whole world knows Piaf. The reason we are still listening to her is because of her extraordinarily powerful voice and because she could convey emotion, which is still felt by everyone who hears her. She speaks across generations and cultures. It is said that to listen to her sing in person was like having someone confess to you and you alone, and people often wept during her performances. You couldn't ignore her; she forced you to share the ups and downs of her universal themes. She paid dearly for her fame, showing the whole world her sordid distress and solitude, pouring her tormented soul and deepest, darkest emotions into her performances to the point where, several times near the end, she almost literally died on stage. She lost consciousness, fell over, couldn't finish shows, cut songs out of her repertoire that were too hard, but never actually died. Her friends witnessed her foaming at the mouth, clinging to the bars of her bed as she demanded her dose of morphine. In fact, near the end of her career, she could only stand up after slamming a syringe of heroin straight through her skirt and stockings and into her leg before going on stage. Some people went to her performances out of a ghoulish fascination to see whether she would make it or not.

• • •

I experienced my own sordid distress, alcohol and dark emotion in an Edith moment when I was nineteen. My brush with mortality came when I inadvertently tried to drink myself to death. I had studied opera and classical singing till I was seventeen then reinvented myself as Joan Baez, listened to Piaf, grew my hair very long and became almost surgically attached to my guitar. Through the folk-singing world I met a wild woman called Barbie. Her honey-blonde hair, flawless skin and deceptively open, angelic face hid a siren. Barbie talked me into a trip down to the South Island that would change my life. She was married and it transpired I was a cover for her real motive, which was to visit her lover. For some reason I ended up alone in the city where we were to stay four days before the siren. I had been given an address to stay at, a huge old mansion of many flats where everyone was interconnected. People lived like that in those days. It was great – full of hippies, students and other refugees from the middle class. We all thought we were fabulous and people smoked dope till it was coming out their wazoos. I knew no one in the house but had been given the name of Ron Moore, who lived in one of the upstairs flats. Barbie's husband had said, 'You can't let her stay with Ron – he'll be awful to her.' But Barbie said, 'No, no, it'll be okay, I'll read Ron the riot act and get someone to keep an eye on her.' Ron was repulsive to me and as predicted acted like I was vermin (couldn't he see I was Joan Baez?), gave me a bottle of whiskey and left me alone in the flat to entertain myself. *What have I done?* I thought, bewildered. *I'm alone in a city I don't know in the custody of a sociopath when I could be having a good time with just about anyone else in the country.* What to do? Why, drink the bottle of whiskey, of course.

My father had taught me to drink whiskey by giving me shot glasses of it cut with water, so whiskey was my friend – what did I know? I just kept drinking and felt fine, but as I wandered around the flat I became more and more miserable, then decided to take a bath. Somehow I got my clothes off, lay in the bath with the bottle of whiskey in my hand and turned the taps on. It felt really good and really soothing. Some time in the middle of the night a man broke into the flat, turned the bath taps off just as I was about to sink unconscious under the water, and dragged me out of the tub. He forced me awake, dried me, put a dressing gown on and walked me up and down the flat for about an hour. During this time I had no idea who I was, the rooms spun uncontrollably, walls closed in and I was in agony. He stuck his finger down my throat to help me vomit, talked calmly and made me keep walking up and down. Eventually, I was able to lie on the bed without falling off, and enjoy the torment of gastric spasms and alcohol poisoning. I knew I was either dead or heading that way, and welcomed obliteration as a respite. While I was contemplating my fall from grace and the psychological ramifications therein, I sunk into unconsciousness.

To my surprise I didn't die. I woke up in the morning wishing I had. Sitting on the bed I asked myself a few basic questions: who are you, where are you, what happened and why do you feel like this? I could only answer the first two, being nineteen, and the most intelligent and helpful thing I could think of was to burst into tears. The man who broke in and saved me had apparently cleaned the bathroom, mopped up the water and left. Hair still clinging damply to my back, I pulled the dressing gown around myself and lurched downstairs to the communal telephone in the hallway. Weeping, I called Barbie to say I was having a horrible time and would be on the first bus out of town. As I turned to crawl upstairs, an Adonis poked his head around the door of one of the other flats.

'Hi,' he said, 'you must be Ron's guest. He told me you were coming – are you okay?'

'No,' I groaned. 'Who are you?'

'I'm the person who dragged you out of the bath last night. Harley.'

I leaned on the stairs. 'What are you talking about?'

'You flooded Ron's bathroom, thus irrigating my kitchen. I think I saved you from drowning.'

I put my hands over my face. He'd seen me naked. Oh God. What else happened? I couldn't quite think what to say next aside from, 'Do you have a stomach pump?'

'I think you had better come in and have a cup of coffee and some aspirin,' he said. Aspirin – so sweet.

I sat down in Harley's lounge feeling like a corpse, drank his coffee, swallowed his aspirin and fell in love with him. Built like a brick shit-house, he was a muscle-bound departure from the skinny folkie intellectuals I hung out with. In the sex appeal and personal magnetism department, I had to admit that Harley was peerless. Sitting across from me in nothing but a pair of cut-off jeans, golden skin warm in the summer morning heat, languid smile mesmerising me, he proceeded to improve on his life-saving performance by revolutionising my life. But that's another story . . .

• • •

Back to Edith. The power of her performances – and don't forget she hardly moved during them and was a tiny black figure alone on the stage with no decorations, video screen or light shows – was drawn from prostitution, the death of her neglected, only child Marcelle, appalling poverty, violent relationships, morphine addiction, alcoholism and constant poor health. Born more or less on the street, she was mostly brought up by her grandmother in a brothel. Her mother deserted her very early on but she had a good if unconventional relationship with her father, who got her singing on the streets very young to help the family finances. Edith adored this life and was out on her own with her step-sister from the age of fifteen. Prostitution is not often alluded to with Piaf but various people told me that she possibly did work the street periodically. That was the world she lived in and a girl had to pay the rent somehow when things were tough and singing wasn't bringing in enough.

Because of her mother's desertion she never ever got over the feeling of being alone and unloved, even though she was always surrounded by friends and hangers-on. Her child died of meningitis while in her boyfriend's care and she was unable to forgive herself. Piaf stayed up all night carousing, drinking and working for the simple reason that she couldn't bear to be alone. She would sleep till the afternoon and begin again. She was tormented by nightmares and even with ear-plugs and eye-masks slept poorly. She never lost her bad habits from the streets – she considered eating properly and personal hygiene to be bourgeois conceits. From young adulthood onwards she suffered with crippling arthritis and gastric ulcers, and eventually died of cancer and cirrhosis of the liver. It was the prescription morphine used to control her pain after a car accident that she couldn't do without. Piaf was really un monstre sacré in every sense of the words, especially in terms of her character. As fabulous and inspiring as she was, she was also violent, temperamental and domineering. Today, she would have been institutionalised as a teenager. She was possibly bipolar, which would have been complicated by suffering from alcoholism from her teens onwards.

Daily from 1951 till the end of her life, Edith was putting huge doses of heroin, morphine, cortisone, alcohol, uppers and downers into her little body just to function. This toxic cocktail blinded a lot of people to her true condition and enabled her to go on stage and give electrifying performances. At her death in 1963 she was only forty-seven but looked like a twisted, tiny, deformed old woman with a ghastly bloated face. The journalist and writer Edward Behr spoke of the last time he saw her. It was in a chic Left Bank nightclub on the rue Saint-Benoît and she looked like a sick, wizened old child. She was balding, her make-up was clownish and she seemed to be unaware of what was going on around her. Her clothes looked like they had been slept in and she looked and smelled unwashed. She seemed exhausted and just sat at the table with a glass of water, seemingly oblivious to the people around her, the noise or her table companions, who included film directors and distinguished song-writers. Behr felt someone should have taken her home, washed her and put her to bed.

● ● ●

Piaf self-destructed because she never got over her terrible childhood, but she always believed in transformation. Because she had been able to transform her own life many times, and had had so many ups and downs, she believed very strongly in helping other people transform theirs. If she saw a poor girl in the street with a malnourished baby, she would give her astronomical sums of money. One girl she did this to actually contacted her years later to thank her, sending her a medal with 'merci' on it – Edith showed this to everyone with pride. She helped the careers of many famous singers, teaching them and giving them spots on her shows – Charles Aznavour, Paul Meurisse, her second husband Jacques Pills, Georges Moustaki, Yves Montand, her third husband Théo Sarapo. For her, transformation was a stronger sensation than drugs or alcohol and to give birth to another star made her drunk with satisfaction. Her attitude to her chaotic personal life was the opposite of her professional life – she was a demonically hard worker, mercilessly forcing herself and her charges to rehearse, sometimes for twelve hours at a stretch. She had an unerring instinct for what would work with a song and on stage. To give you an idea of her professionalism, the great love of her life was the boxer Marcel Cerdan, who was killed in a plane crash on his way to see her in the United States. In spite of crippling grief, she got up on stage the night he died and completed a concert dedicated to him. She collapsed as soon as she left the stage.

• • •

To get back to my apartment on the rue de la Castre in Cannes, I opened the black iron gate, tottered across a little bridge, opened the outside door, walked down a short passage and opened my front door. Once upstairs, I would sit facing the windows, which opened out onto the tiled rooftops of the Suquet, the unadulterated blue sky and huge gulls who asked me loudly what I was doing and why I wasn't feeding them. I played Jacques Brel and Piaf CDs in my laptop as I wrote, drank iced rosé, ate olives and let the conversations from the street waft up to my third-floor gaff. Well, actually I thought it was a palace because it had more than one room and it was all mine.

One evening I was invited to dine at the home of Robert, the chauffeur my friends in Roquefort-les-Pins use when they are in Cannes. His apartment was in central Cannes on the fourth floor of an imposing Art Deco building. I rattled up in the antique see-through lift clutching my bottle of Bandol rosé and was ushered into an airy, white, Italianesque mini palace with pale Italian tiles, French doors opening out to balconies from every window, antique furniture and Robert's wife Danielle in gold slippers. Piaf was playing on the sound system. As we moved to the main balcony to take in the sparkling view of the luxury launches and yachts by night, I thought, *All this and he's a chauffeur and she's a part-time pharmacy assistant!* A sprightly man in his fifties, Robert assured me they had bought and decorated this apartment with pure unadulterated sweat. When I described this luxurious pad of a chauffeur to my Parisian friends, they assured me I was being ludicrously naïve if I accepted his 'hard work' explanation for his wealth. In their opinion he was sure to have gangster connections because everyone did in Cannes. The two other guests that evening were an ancient German heiress and her dame de compagnie, whom Robert called the lovebirds. I don't think they were gangsters. In spite of their formal manners and grand station in life, Robert behaved like a typical Meridional with them: relaxed, laughing and talking non-stop, loosening his trousers when he had eaten too much of his beautiful wife's cuisine, taking his shirt off when the heat got too much and lying on the couch while Danielle did everything. Afterwards, we all got a ride home in Danielle's huge silver Mercedes.

• • •

Piaf was not afraid to attack forbidden subjects. She sang about drug addiction, violence, self-pity, forbidden love and even suicide. In 'Les Amants d'Un Jour' – 'Lovers For a Day' – she tells the story of a hard-bitten old waitress who can't bear sentimentality but, if pressed, will admit that she once met a tragic couple who brought sunshine into her life for just one day. Star-crossed lovers, they had come to the hotel where she was working, to die together. They arrived hand in hand, asking for a sunny room where they were later found, still hand in hand with the sun pouring in on them, their eyes closed against the morrow. It hurt her to see them, but at the same time they were so happy that their love entered her heart and she felt full of sunshine.

Her last lover and husband was a man twenty years

her junior, Théo Sarapo. She tried to turn him into a singer and they did actually record a very charming song together, 'A Quoi Ça Sert l'Amour?' – 'What's the Point of Love?' – sung in a question and answer sequence. He is asking what the point of love is and she is explaining that it's there to give us joy. As usual she is telling him he is the one, the last one, the only one and this is the power of love. She was a martyr to doomed love. Two months after marrying him, she fell into a coma. Théo had taken her down to the villa in Plascassier, hoping it would do her some good, but she slipped in and out of consciousness and finally died on 11 October 1963, dying on the same day as her old friend Jean Cocteau. Two days before her death she told her half-sister Simone she was getting ready for a series of performances. Théo secretly drove her body back to Paris because he didn't want the world to know she hadn't died there, where she really belonged. When France found out, consumed with grief, a hundred thousand people came to her funeral at Père Lachaise cemetery in Paris. Traffic in Paris came to a stop. Her hearse was followed by eleven limousines covered in wreaths, the hugest from the Foreign Legion. Everyone was there – Marlene Dietrich, music-hall stars, soldiers, prostitutes, pimps, local working-class people, students – all the people who felt she had sung specially for them.

Arrêtez! Arrêtez la musique!
Stop! Stop the music!

Tattooed Lady

> Your body is a temple, but how long
> can you live in the same house before
> you redecorate?
>
> *Anonymous*

'Vajazzling,' said the nice man opposite me in the restaurant.

'I beg your pardon?'

'It's called vajazzling,' he repeated, feeding himself another mouthful of twelve-hour lamb. 'Female genital decorating is called vajazzling. It's all the rage in Los Angeles.'

'What did he say?' my friend next to me asked.

'You don't want to know. Eat your fish and think pure thoughts. All I did was ask if anyone knew about genital tattooing.'

'Yes,' said the nice man, 'you can get all sorts of stuff done like Swarovski crystals, glitter, jewels.'

'How do you know that?' I asked him.

'I just know,' he smiled. This man's speciality is genetic engineering – how could he have such connoisseur information that no woman at the table had?

Earlier in the week I had been sitting in a bar with my friend Dorothy telling her I was looking for a really exciting story for this book. We drank some more wine, looked around and our eyes fell on the barmaid. She had her arms tattooed from her hands to just above her elbows. It was a beautiful design of winding leaves on the outside of her arm and religious icons on the inside. Dorothy said, 'Why don't you write on tattooing – the ultimate transformation story?' Altering the surface of the skin from one thing to another thing. I had never had any interest in tattoos or tattooed people except to think, *When that girl with the beautiful smooth skin and exhibitionist tendencies turns sixty, that faded tattoo is going to look so bad on her withered arm.* I liked the idea of women acquiring a small hidden secret tattoo that would only be visible to a lover, but found large visible tattoos on men and women absolutely terrifying – it seemed like such an aggressive thing to do. I didn't comprehend how they could withstand the relentless attention – you would always be the tattooed lady, not Jocelyn from Grey Lynn who had a brain, ate bacon-and-egg pie and was nice to her nana. Bad enough having red hair and a loud voice, but a full body tattoo? My second thought was always, *How are they going to get it off when they've changed their mind?* These questions plagued me, but it wasn't till I turned up at the tattoo studio in my neighbourhood that I realised I had approximately 300 more queries.

Two Hands Tattoo is the chic face of tattooing. The black-and-white entrance to the upstairs-flat-turned-tattoo-studio is cute and stylish. You climb the stairs to what could be a funky dentist's office of several rooms: polished wooden floors, clean white walls covered with beautiful paintings, drawings and photos and the faint noise of drills. I walked in nervously with no appointment, introduced myself and tried to look funky. A very sweet young man with an angelic open face, fair Irish skin, short curly hair, earlobe plugs and tattoos was at work on a client reclined on a bed. Victor Valour is the tattooist's name and he invited me to sit in on the session. He and his client would both be happy to answer my questions. I admit I was a bit disappointed, expecting as I was whores, gangsters, ne'er-do-wells and sailors drinking rum. I expected the place to smell of alcohol, cigarettes, sweat and fear. I thought the walls would be oozing pain. The client was a chef and looking very relaxed as the ink was being drilled into the length of his arm.

'Doesn't that hurt?' I asked.

'Not really. It's like being stung or pinged with a rubber band, but I wouldn't call it pain. This method of electric pen is much less painful than the traditional chisel method the Polynesians used.'

I knew that around 1769 Captain Cook's sailors had been tattooed by Māori when they visited New Zealand and had taken the art back to England, where it became rather fashionable. When I visited the Captain Cook Memorial Museum in Whitby I saw the tattooing instruments and also gruesome tattooed dried heads. Growing up in New Zealand we had always seen Māori elders, both men and women, with moko or whakairo – facial tattooing. They didn't have the smooth silky inking you see now but actual grooves in their faces, like carving. This was a very painful process wherein the skin was not pricked with bone needles but actually carved with a little non-serrated bone chisel, called a uhi, to produce grooves. The grooves were then filled in with pigment, soot or charcoal powder by a serrated chisel. This hasn't been the method of choice since 1925, and in 1910 darning needles were introduced for moko.

The word tattoo comes from the Tahitian 'tatau', meaning to mark. The word 'whakairo' really refers to woodcarving and then came to be used for skin carving. Polynesians used a wide comb like an adze, which was dipped in pigment, put on the skin and driven in with a mallet. If you wanted more refined detail you would use a smaller comb. Tattooing was done to signify rank and social status; a warrior could earn it or it might have religious significance. You might also be tattooed as a slave or a low-class person. These tattoos were usually on the back and included mistakes to show that you were nobody. The Māori originally preserved the tattooed heads of chiefs when they died as a mark of respect. These dried heads were very highly valued by Māori and later European settlers, who were fascinated by them, wanted to buy them. The two started trading heads for guns, but the demand was so great for both that Māori provided the heads of their enemies and eventually, rumour has it, actually murdered men for their tattooed heads. Sometimes slaves were tattooed then beheaded for the trade. Gruesome.

Māori women mostly had their chin, philtrum (space between the upper lip and the nose) and lips (and sometimes the inside of their lips) tattooed with blue dye. Usually only women and girls of rank had the right to be tattooed and it was performed by a tohunga (expert). They would advise their fathers or brothers that they wished to have it done and the payment of food delicacies was collected – hūia birds, kiwi, kākāpō, rats, fish, ferns, et cetera. Upon completion the women had albatross skin placed in their ears and were dressed with head feathers and ceremonial cloaks. Really, females could get a tattoo in all sorts of places – the forehead, between the eyebrows, nose, neck, breast, stomach, genitals, shoulders, back and legs. But it was unusual. White missionaries at the time found the tattooing of women to be barbarous devil's art and made great efforts to put a stop to it. Tattooing on men died out by the late 1800s, mostly because there were no more wars. Interestingly, the opposite happened with female tattooing, which experienced a surge, especially on the chin and lips. As Māori drifted to the cities to work in the early 1900s, women had it done to assert identity and whakapapa (genealogy). Tattooing for Māori has undergone a revival. My tattooist, Victor, had his done in the traditional way with a chisel.

As I was writing this piece it became clear that I had to get a tattoo done on myself. I needed to experience inking so I could understand why people did it (particularly women), how it felt and how I would feel about it afterwards. So I made an appointment with Victor and went into Two Hands to draw up some ideas with him. I wanted something small, meaningful and more or less hidden, visible only if I went swimming. I was vacillating between a rose and a Moroccan henna-style tattoo. In the end I settled on a pink rose with the words 'La Vie en Rose' written around it. I chose this because of my love of Edith Piaf songs and because, in spite of everything, I *do* see life through rose-tinted glasses. We then made an appointment to do the deed and I returned the following Thursday with my producer Jane and her son Angus, present for support and photos. Victor got me to approve the drawing, made a stencil of it and asked me to reveal my shoulder. The skin was cleaned with alcohol and the stencil applied. I lay face down on the bed while he removed the needles and applicator from their autoclaved packets then filled tiny plastic pots with different-coloured inks. Finally everything was ready and Victor hit the electricity to make the needle turn into a drill.

The original tattooing machine is based on the design of the doorbell. The staccato action of poking ink into the skin is powered by a circuit just like a doorbell. If you're in prison you can make a tattoo machine from guitar strings and a tape-deck motor. Up until that point I had, for some reason, convinced myself that tattooing *would* in fact feel like a sting or a rubber band pinging, but as soon as I heard the sound of the drill I realised that putting a drill onto my tender girl skin was going to hurt. I looked at the man on the other side of the room getting a giant tattoo on his chest and he was just lying there calmly, not gnashing his teeth, not twisting, not grunting in agony. Afterwards, I asked him how he could look so calm in the face of such torture and he replied he was being staunch because I was there.

I put my head on the rubber head-rest, smiled confidently at Jane and allowed a young man to drill lines into my flesh. It felt exactly like what it was – a sharp instrument gouging my skin. It went on for twenty minutes with two breaks for me to breathe. The outline of the rose and the words were done first with a non-serrated needle, then it was swapped for a finer, serrated one for filling in the colours. 'Let's just leave it with the outline and forget the filling,' I begged. Clenching and unclenching my fists, groaning occasionally and talking to Victor and Jane provided distraction, but didn't stop the pain. 'It's not *that* bad,' said Victor cheerfully. 'Oh right – blame the victim.' I thought it couldn't be as bad as getting Botox, but it almost was. When it was over Victor washed the rose with soapy water, let me look at the reddened area around the tattoo (which I could hardly make out through all my freckles), slapped petroleum jelly on and covered it with plastic wrap and Sellotape. Victor's post-op instructions were to wash the tattoo with soapy water every day and keep putting a non-perfumed cream on it. My post-op instructions were to smoke the joint I should have smoked pre-op and go straight to the nearest bar. Which is exactly what Jane, Angus and I did. And two cosmopolitans in quick succession later, I felt slightly better. It was a little stingy for the rest of the day, didn't bother me at all during the night and within a few days I had forgotten about it.

When friends heard I had a tattoo they all said, 'Does your mother know?' to which I would reply, 'I'm sixty-two years old', to which they would say, 'Yeah, but I know your mother.'

In fact, my first experience of tattooing was of my mother's tattoo. It was on her face and no one knew it was a tattoo – not her husband, not her children, not her friends. Aged fifty she had it removed because she decided she was too old for it. When she was in her twenties in the Royal Australian Navy, her naughty friend Mickey had talked her into getting a little tattoo with her. They would do it together to give themselves the courage to go through with it. My mother went in first and had a little beauty spot tattooed on her cheekbone. Mickey chickened out, so the good girl of the two of them was left with a blue beauty spot forever. My mother has high cheekbones, so the beauty spot looked gorgeous. When she went to have it removed, the doctor said, 'You know it's not unusual to have a blue mole.' 'It's not a mole,' said my very bourgeois, round-vowel-speaking mother. Of course this generation thinks it invented body decorating, but my mother and her Navy friends drew lines up the backs of their legs to simulate the seam of silk stockings, painted butterflies on finger nails and had blonde streaks dyed into their hair.

• • •

When I asked the guys at Two Hands about genital tattooing, the white men said they didn't know and the brown ones nearly died of embarrassment, so I decided to find out elsewhere. It turns out Māori women did sometimes have genital tattoos, but it was unusual. The late-nineteenth-century chieftainess Rangi Te Apakura had one on her mons veneris. In a Māori song written about this tattoo the words go: 'Lest the struggles of Tutaeahua succeed they will be stopped secretly by the tattoo marks of the vagina of Rangi Te Apakura'. Choice.

Just the thought of this makes me want to cross my legs forever. Nevertheless, I looked a bit more into the sparkling cult of vajazzling. I should say in advance that neither genital tattooing nor vajazzling is normally done on the labia – it stops before at the mons. The technical definition is 'The act of applying glitter and jewels to a woman's nether regions for aesthetic purposes.' Seems like a lot of work for nothing to me because (a) no one sees it and (b) the one person who might is likely to be a man and the last person who would be interested in it would be a man. Men don't notice clothes, shoes or sexy underwear, so why would they be interested in getting a crystal up their wazoo, down their throat or in their hair? I can see it for Christmas or Guy Fawkes, but not for Easter. Wait, I've just thought of trick or treat! Maybe it's a woman on woman thing. You can get bejewelled up your tummy and on your breasts too, which is rather beautiful. The glue is just like any other glue you would use to stick things on your body, like eyelashes. It pulls off easily. Supposedly they stay stuck for up to five days, but how do you wash? One guy said when his girlfriend had it done he was finding glitter all over the house for days; he even had a jewel embedded in his butt, and no, you're not allowed to ask how that happened. If you are inked you can jazz up your tattoos with some sparkles.

This leads me to the scandalous Edwardians who not only indulged in tattooing but also nipple piercing. The most famous Edwardian to get inked was the Prince of Wales, subsequently to become King Edward VII, who got a Cross of Jerusalem pricked onto his arm when he was visiting the Holy Land in 1862. His son, the Duke of York (later King George V), did the same thing twenty years later in Japan when he got a dragon inked on. Lady Randolph Churchill, the mother of Winston Churchill, had a thin snake tattooed around her wrist, which she hid with a bracelet. Women also had cosmetic tattooing done on their faces – cheeks for rouge and lips for outline, et cetera. We tend to think of tattooing in the past as the realm of convicts or sailors, but it was actually very fashionable and expensive to get inked in those days, which is why it was mostly the domain of the aristocracy. When Edwardian women had piercings, they often attached a dainty chain between the nipples and were convinced that the piercing improved the fullness and firmness of the breasts. The description in Stephen Kern's book *Anatomy and Destiny* is dire. It was normally done by two women: one would place her arm around the client's neck and hold her firmly; the other one would disinfect the nipple then clamp a tong with two fine tubes onto the nipple and screw it in place. Using the tubes as a guide, the piercer was quickly inserted between them and through the nipple. Then the ring was passed through and closed. Cripes.

The wonderful thing about modern tattooing is that it can be extraordinarily beautiful, whimsical and funny. There seems to be an affinity between foodies and tattooing in terms of self-expression and transformation. Lots of well-known chefs have contemporary tattoos, but what I didn't know is they can include coffee, tomatoes, lamingtons, herbs, a row of designer lettuces, pork terrine, lobsters, knives and forks, a bottle of Beaujolais, jelly beans . . . a female chef in Melbourne has I'M HUNGRY tattooed on her inner bottom lip. The possibilities are endless. If you are a man you could have a box of baking powder tattooed on your lower abdomen with the helpful words SURE TO RISE. If you are a woman you could have a lamb chop on your bottom with the truthful words FAT IS DELICIOUS. Now I regret just getting a boring old rose, but then again a rose is a rose is a rose. I could have had a Laguiole knife with a lime-green handle inked onto my forearm.

At the same dinner where I found out about vajazzling I met a man called Bryce, who has lots of tattoos. Like a lot of people, his first tattoo was his lover's initials, which he then covered up with a midnight sun. It was inspired by Sarah Vaughan singing 'I could see the midnight sun . . .

Was there such a light? It's a thrill I still don't quite believe
. . . stardust on my sleeve'. His third tattoo is a manaia,
the creature in Māori folktales that lives halfway between
heaven and earth. It's a copy of a bone carving that a dear
friend gave him, which he found very claustrophobic to
wear around the neck, so now it's a tattoo on his shoulder
blade – done by a Mexican in Hackney. Bryce was such a
good storyteller, I asked him about the rest.

Bryce: My fourth and fifth tattoos are a set of
wings, down each arm and across my shoulder
and towards my clavicle. I thought a lot about
a symbol that spoke to me about having been
away from New Zealand and coming back after
twenty-two years. The symbol came to me as I
was travelling around Brazil, on my way home. If
I think about it now, it's funny that I chose wings
to symbolise returning home. I think that I will
always have an urge to fly away, although I'm
teaching myself to live more in the present. I've
only just this summer, after having my full set
of tattoos for the last five years, started to wear
singlets that show them. I can cover them up
easily with shirt sleeves, which is what I wanted
to do at work. They used to be very private to
me and to the one long-term lover I've had in
the last five years, but now I am single, I don't
mind going round the house, down to the shops,

to the beach, the gym, with them being visible. Also, they are in places where the skin won't sag with age. They have become much less than just a part of my sexual being, and much more a part of my overall self. My mother really likes them. Some friends won't even mention them, others are fine. My nieces love them; my daughter hates them. It's individual to them.

Peta: Is there a sexual element to tattooing?

Bryce: Yes, definitely. I had a lover who was very important to me, sexually and emotionally, and he was the only one who saw the wings after they had been completed and it was private to him for a couple of years. I think that I'm much more easy and open about people seeing them because I'm no longer under his spell. The first few weeks of going around with them being visible was quite a revelation. Not about what other people thought – after all, we are quite a tattooed nation – but how I felt about exposing myself when it used to be so private.

Peta: What next?

Bryce: Something will happen – it's kind of taking shape in my head and it's something to do with an exploding flower. I'll think about it some more and then act on it. But it would also be nice to celebrate a new lover with a tattoo and keep it private for as long as the love lasts . . .

In terms of ancient tattooing, there are many cultural traditions. The oldest records are of Egyptian body-marking dating back 4500 years. Even though they are the oldest records, the Egyptians got the technique from the Nubians. The original ones were dots and dashes and were almost exclusively done on women. Some of the tattoos were in the pubic area, suggesting an erotic overtone. The Egyptians also branded slaves and prisoners of war. There is a female mummy in a museum in Peru showing delicate spiral tattooing on her fingers. They used two kinds of instrument: one was a wood-handled stick with a very sharp point and the other was a bronze tool with needles at the end. The tip was dipped in a mixture of breast milk and soot, which was rubbed into the wounds.

Africa has long indulged in body-marking, either tattooing or scarification, for various reasons. In women in particular it was done for the sensual and erotic feeling of touching them, to denote personal qualities, to show history and cultural status and to prove you were a civilised individual. Because the skin of Africans is so dark, they often specialised in cutting and scarring, which showed up better. According to the book *Marks of Civilization*, raised spots and lines of relief were engraved onto the skin to make the human body perfect. They didn't consider the human body to be beautiful until it had been fixed up with tattoos and scars. To produce what is called 'keloids' or raised scars, you use a razor blade to cut the skin, which is pinched up with an acacia thorn, fishhook or arrowhead. You then rub the incision with soot or clay which irritates the wound and stops it from healing properly, thus developing permanent bumps. This is a very painful process and sometimes results in infection, but it looks impressive.

The Japanese were tattooing very early on – probably since the sixth century. Initially it was done for punishment and commonly applied around the eyes. Later, mouth, hand and arm tattoos were observed on women. In the late fifteenth century it became the domain of the samurai warrior. Modern Japanese tattooing was done on courtesans as a love pledge – their lover's names would be found on the inner thigh or upper arm. As tattooing had always been considered criminal, the authorities of the time were horrified that both men and women were using it as a form of decoration. The authorities thought tattoos common and indecent, but the folk who wore them considered themselves to be roguishly sexy. From the late eighteenth century onwards, still underground, tattooing moved from just being marks to being images that depicted a story. It was a kind of resistance to authority and was associated with rowdy, low-class people. From about 1886, while the authorities were still trying to suppress tattooing, visiting Europeans were fascinated (notably George V and Nicholas II) and falling over themselves to get inked in the ports of Kobe and Yokohama. After World War Two, tattooing finally became legal in Japan and these days there is quite a strong erotic and sadomasochistic element to it.

The Japanese full-body tattoos are very beautiful and include dragons, samurai warriors, Buddhist deities, serpents, flowers, animals and swords. Traditional tattooing is severely painful and requires great fortitude and patience on the part of both the practitioner and the client. The ink used to be a special charcoal ink which turned blue/green under the skin. It is done by hand with no mallet to force the needles in, so you can imagine the skill required of the 'master'. He holds a long slim tool in his hand as if he was stoking a fire or holding a pencil. It is made from bamboo and steel with a tight bunch of fine needles fastened at the end. The client lies on the floor, the master sits cross-legged by him. He dips the instrument in the ink, stretches the skin with his free hand and punctures it repeatedly with the hand holding the instrument. According to the Japanese masters, this precision technique is much less damaging to tissue than any modern method and achieves just as pure a result.

The Nepalese, Indians and North Africans did very beautiful tattooing, particularly on women. Sometimes in Morocco, where I go every year, I still see old women in the hammam (bath house) with inking on their chins, foreheads and around their eyes. They also used to do it on hands, arms, feet, chests and necks. They were originally inked for decoration and good luck, but at the beginning of the colonial period facial decorating was gradually replaced by lipstick and an unmarked face was considered more civilised. Interestingly, Islam forbade tattooing and men never did it, but the women insisted on continuing because pre-Islam they had always done it. These days it is replaced by henna marking, which also has an ancient history, originally coming from India and travelling through the Middle East to Arab countries. Tattooing probably arrived by the same route because both art forms were often used together.

The most fascinating story of all, though, comes from Alaska. Inuit and Aleut people decorated their faces in a very unusual way, which I only came across by chance. No living person has ever seen this tattooing because the missionaries wiped it out. They combined tattooing on their faces with permanently inserted bits of bone or stone (labrets) to which they attached strands of beads (for special occasions). These beads hung down over the mouth and chin like little curtains. They also inserted cheek and lip plugs; oblong winged labrets through the nose and parallel to the lips; shells, coral, glass and amber. Now I know why they didn't kiss with their lips – they pressed the nose against the other person's cheek or forehead and breathed in so that the person's hair and skin came up against theirs. It was a platonic kiss, not a sexual one. Parents actually started making cuts for labrets and holes in the septum of the nose when their children were babies. Needless to say, if you got labrets inserted as an adolescent it hurt like hell, so they clenched pieces of wood between the teeth to control the pain.

The last inevitable question remains – how do you erase a tattoo you regret? How do you erase JONNIE FOREVER when you ripped Jonnie out of your heart years ago? Tattoos don't come off easily – the 5000-year-old frozen man Ötzi, found in Italy in 1991, had fifty-seven tattoos and they were all still there! They were lines and dots, which have been interpreted as being for medicinal purposes, like guides for acupuncture. In the old days the missionaries tried to get rid of Polynesian tattoos by 'holystoning' or sand-stoning – rubbing the skin with stone. Needless to say this method did not remove tattoos as they are not on the surface of the skin, but it did produce a lot of suffering and damage. People have tried bleach, lemon juice, lightening creams, salt and covering up with another tattoo. Then dermabrasion was used, in which the skin is anaesthetised then electronically sanded. This produces bleeding and loss of plasma and takes weeks to recover from. You could also have the tattoo excised, in which a small tattoo would be cut out and the skin sutured together again. For a big tattoo you would have a skin graft. Both leave scars. These days laser removal is popular – light is lasered onto the tattoo and the body assimilates the ink internally. It does leave blisters and some scarring. The most successful method seems to be light therapy, which is more sophisticated than ordinary laser but a lot more expensive and leaves minimal scarring.

The most revealing thing I found out about tattooing is that it can become addictive. In Rachael King's book

Magpie Hall, one of the female characters, Dora, originally wanted to get a tattoo as a bonding ritual with her husband, who she discovers on their wedding night is inked all over. The story is set in New Zealand in the late 1800s. Rather than being horrified by his tattoos, she is fascinated. Inexorably, she is drawn again and again to the seedy tattoo parlour down by the docks for various reasons – he is away a lot and she misses him, the pain excites her, it binds her to her love forever, it thrills her sexually and makes her feel vital and alive in her restricted life. Dora goes back and back for butterflies, shells, birds and flowers; she wants to be covered in love tattoos and to sink into this mysterious world of inking.

In terms of my own rose tattoo, I can't say it has been a transformation story. I did it out of interest, haven't turned out to be addicted and because it is on my back, never think about it. I just see it as another form of make-up, albeit permanent. In ancient cultures tattooing had a strong purpose, telling a story of rank, place and history. You were considered ugly and 'unwritten' without one. These days tattooing really does seem to be life-changing in the sense that people have meaningful tattoos put on their bodies – they mean them to stay there and they wish them to communicate a story. It has not only become very fashionable, but indeed addictive.

How to Buy Hope

From the age of zero to eighteen a girl
needs good parents.
From the age of eighteen to twenty-five a
girl needs good looks.
From the age of twenty-five to fifty a girl
needs a good personality.
And from fifty onwards a girl needs cash.

Joan Collins

Can we talk? I can't stand people who say it's great to be
older, great to be wise, not care what people think, be
freer, more philosophical, blah blah blah. Don't they have
mirrors? Don't they ever leave the house? Don't they know
nature is trying to get rid of them? In my book on women,
Can We Help It If We're Fabulous?, I said there's nothing to
be gained from being natural, trusting nature and letting
nature take its course. NATURE IS YOUR ENEMY – she

wants to get rid of women as soon as our first blush of youth is over. She bends over backwards to make our female bones brittle, drives us insane by withdrawing essential hormones, makes our skin look like a snake's and prevents us from sleeping properly. As soon as we're not needed any more to reproduce and attract breeding partners, she takes away our looks, our strength – our relevance. Nature couldn't give a stuff about us – we have to look after ourselves. The only reason we live to ninety is because of medical advances, the only reason we can see is because of glasses, and the only reason we don't starve is because the state looks after us. Well it does now, but who knows if it will next week. Old age goes on for a long time – best to be as fit and healthy as possible. Obviously nature wins in the end, but you should at least go down fighting with moisturised skin.

I always used to think there would be a moment in my life when I realised I had 'got it'. I don't know what age I thought that might be – forty maybe? Fifty? When I was young I used to say, 'If I haven't made it by the time I'm thirty, I'm going to kill myself.' Then it was, 'Okay, so if I haven't made it by forty, I am really going to kill myself.' This is the brain of a slack Type-A person who wants to achieve but on the other hand is having too good a time and making too many dumb mistakes to actually do it. I can't stand people who say they have no regrets. How can you have no regrets? Don't you regret not going to Paris when you could have? Don't you regret choosing the wrong husband? Twice. Don't you regret renting all those years when you should've bitten the bullet and bought? Don't you regret having too many children? Don't you regret that bad investment? I can't stand starry-eyed, cliché-ridden, pathologically selective-memory older people who say life starts at forty, fifty, sixty, whatever. No it doesn't. Life starts when you're born and you just make the best of it, for better or for worse. And you restart it lots of times when you lose everything. Most of it is luck – not good management as these useless books on getting older tell you.

● ● ●

My ninety-two-year-old mother has assured me reaching that age isn't all it's cracked up to be – the person you end up having the closest relationship with is your doctor. It's mostly maintenance and cheating and preventing the rot that leads to our inevitable fate. Life is just one goddamn thing after another; you do all that work and then you don't even get out of it alive. My mother didn't say that but that's what she means. Thankfully my parents don't bang on about the joys of getting older – I'm a chip off the now brittle block – they just look after themselves, take the medication and make jokes about how ghastly it is. They have all sorts of things wrong with them, but no heart disease, no cancer, no dementia and no strokes – incredibly.

When I turned sixty I decided *not* to ignore it and then take all my sleeping pills in one go. I decided to draw attention to it, have a huge party, make people pay to come, then give all the money away to charity. I got some gay guys to do my make-up and hair, put on a fabulous gown and gave people a big fat opportunity to say CAN YOU BELIEVE SHE'S SIXTY?! And she still has moisturised skin and she can still sing and she can still stand up. They say age only matters if you are a cheese, but it's pretty traumatic when you turn sixty – much worse than waking up as cheese. I started glorifying my October birthday well in advance in Marrakech, continued on in Paris and ended it in Auckland. And it's not over yet – I'll continue profiting from it till the next birthday, at which point I will start celebrating that I'm not sixty.

• • •

Having a party in Marrakech is always a good idea because you just say the word 'party' and Moroccans immediately throw themselves into cooking and planning in their mad, over-crowded, passionate way. I was staying at Hotel du Tresor, the place I always stay, and the owner Adriano decided to throw my party on the top terrace where it's not so hot and you have a view of the medina. The staff would organise everything – all I had to do was turn up. So I sat on my bed sipping mint tea and listening to the dusk chorus of birds in the huge orange tree reaching right up through the riad. As is normal in Morocco, the cook, who is a woman, had spent all afternoon preparing a traditional Moroccan meal and cakes, and the staff, who are men, had done nothing. This is a standard division of labour in Morocco. The situation was remedied by Adriano throwing a wobbly and within half an hour drinks, glasses, table settings and uniformed male staff appeared. 'She's sixty!' he shouted. 'She comes from an island in the South Pacific and they celebrate that there!'

To contribute to the air of confusion and drama, the ring road around Marrakech was closed off so half the guests arrived late, the staff who didn't drink got drunk, the traditional musicians got very stoned, one friend had an emotional crisis and had to be picked up after collapsing in tears, people no one had ever seen before turned up and everyone said right on cue, 'You CAN'T be sixty!' I got a fake diamond ring from one of the male staff who spent all day blowing me kisses and clutching his heart. Adriano's eighty-year-old Italian mother turned up, dressed from head to toe in Christian Lacroix. I said, 'I want your outfit' (she's about 4 foot 11 and the size of a toothpick). She said, 'Well you'll need to lose weight and I'll need to die, but the chances are you won't get this dress any time soon.' Morocco is a major grower of roses, so I received bunches and bunches of them, insisted on sleeping with them, almost died of carbon monoxide poisoning and woke up to what closely resembled a funeral parlour.

Following that, the Paris birthday party was kind of a moveable feast. My greatest stretch of exercise involves walking to the wine shop and back, so if I can cycle around Paris for four hours at sixty years of age, anyone can. It's quite fab doing something you would hesitate to do even in a car; pedalling around terrifying Paris on your birthday is liberating and euphoria-producing. You are in an organised group, so protected by other spatially challenged people; the guide tells you all about the Petit Palais, the Grand Palais, the Tuileries and the Pont Neuf, so you get your culture hit; and you even get to stop for lunch, order a crêpe in colourful français and throw back un ballon de rouge.

One of the best bistros in Paris is right at the Métro Odéon, and you can't get in unless you promise your first-born son or lie down on the pavement and say you're sinking into a diabetic coma. Or say it's your birthday. I grabbed an Australian couple's baby and shouted, 'The kid's suffering from dehydration – we need liquids immediately.' This seemed to work. In no time the queue (yes, queue!) had reduced itself to just my friends and I, and soon we were mainlining foie gras, home-made charcuterie and heavenly country bread. I am extremely reluctant to give you this information, thus causing competition for my front-line table, one glass of wine away from the pavement, but here it is – the place is called Le Comptoir du Relais. The madly delicious food is the brainchild of the famous haute cuisine chef, Yves

Camdeborde. The food is traditional cuisine du terroir, regional cooking, resplendent with earthy pigs' trotters, lentil soup with soft sheep-milk cheese, pork terrine, beef cheeks, fabulous cheese platter and a great wine list full of small producers. My Paris friends come here for the boiled eggs with mayonnaise, maintaining they are the best in Paris. Even the staff are brilliant and charming – unheard of in snippy-snappy Paris. When we finished I asked the waiter if he was leaving too; he said, 'Pas sans vous' – not without you.

When you know Paris quite well, you are always looking for something different or quirky, especially on your birthday. How many times do you want to drag yourself through the Louvre anyway? How many times do you turn sixty anyway? So I went online and discovered a smart and interesting website called mylittleparis.com, which not only gives gastronomic but culture, fashion, household and luxury information as well. People in the know in Paris are in love with heritage tomatoes – the uglier and the weirder the better. Some enterprising slow food people have set up a company called Terroirs d'Avenir to help foodies access top-of-the-line edibles from small producers. It's all terribly cloak and dagger and Parisians can only get their hands on the best asparagus, tomatoes, fish, strawberries or whatever's in season once a month on a Saturday. Devotees are only told hours ahead where the secret pick-up location is. I almost died of excitement before I even got there. On my birthday it happened to be a crate of heritage tomatoes to be picked up from Frenchie, a very 'in' little bistro in the 2nd arrondissement, where I got to try some of them on bruschetta with a glass of wine.

• • •

When I got back to Auckland, the planning for the big charity birthday bash to raise funds for multiple sclerosis research was well under way. A party in New Zealand is the opposite of a party in Morocco. The Multiple Sclerosis Society had printed invitations, information sheets, run sheets, production sheets, had organised slick catering, lighting, sound, and found an unbelievable location at the top of the Auckland War Memorial Museum. They had been organising this for months – so on the night, when they said Brazilian samba dancers on at 7.50 p.m., Peta to talk 8.32 p.m., Buckwheat on at 10.01 p.m., that's *exactly* what happened. The Bollywood dancers, opera singer and rock band all performed brilliantly, as predestined. The food was perfect, the cake was five foot high and lots of money was raised for MS. My family came over from Australia. Because you can't kill weeds, the mother didn't want to go home and my brothers and sisters were the last to leave. The dress theme was 1970s and my personal prize for best dressed went to my friend Cathy, who wore a huge blonde wig, dark glasses and shocking pink go-go outfit. She also had very moisturised skin.

The other day I had the yearly appointment with my accountant, which is like the end-of-the-year audience with the head nun at school. I get exactly the same feeling of dread. I know she's going to say, 'You earned too much money – now look at all the tax you're going to have to pay.' Then she'll say, 'You spent too much money – when are you going to grow up?' Then we'll talk about her family and my friends and shoes and hairdos and the meaning of life. But this time I actually looked at her ghastly lists of what I had spent on what, and there it was in black and white: GROOMING $8,240.05. Eight thousand, two hundred and forty dollars! In one year. Further down was what I had spent on rent living in the south of France for five months – more or less the same amount. I had spent the same sum on rent as I had on my appearance. I stood up and looked in the mirror and thought, *Was it worth it? I could have reduced my mortgage with that and I still look like a wreck.*

My point is, it costs a lot just keeping your act together, which is why this essay is called 'How to Buy Hope'. When you're young, your grooming consists of getting out of bed, washing your face, brushing your hair and getting on with the day. Or sleeping on the beach, bypassing hair and washing, and getting on with the day. You look fabulous because you are twenty-five – your hair is thick and shiny, your skin is clear and tight, you are a normal weight and you've never even heard of the term 'chicken-neck'. I never used body cream, ever. Who knew the perfect skin on your stomach would end up looking like blancmange?

Outraged at my accountant's miscalculations and blatant lies, I demanded a breakdown of this grooming sum. She burst out laughing and said, 'What do you think it is, Peta? Dentist, doctor, make-up, hairdresser, massage, osteopath, skin cream, Botox, shampoo and conditioner, yoga, clothes, shoes, et cetera, et cetera.' I called my friend Verna and she said, 'What? Only eight and a half grand? You're an underachiever – you need to double it.'

'But we're not talking facelifts, liposuction or hip surgery here. We're talking ordinary grooming.'

'You don't need designer clothes.'

'But I *do* – for my mental health. Marni just falls better than Top Shop.'

'You need to add pedicures, Restylane, facials and the gym.'

Who needs the gym with this endless dance going on? The dance of keeping up appearances, that is. When I wrote that no woman over thirty should leave the house without lipstick on, I got a letter of complaint from a woman who said lipstick looked awful on older women. She also complained about my hair on television and said she hoped someone 'of consequence' would come along and sort me out. She personally blamed it all on men – I was doing it to please some no-good man. Damn right – the postman, the gardener, the plumber, the electrician and the dog. Why frighten innocent people who've done nothing but walk by your window? Here's my look for when I go swimming daily at my neighbourhood beach: eyebrow pencil, lipstick, tinted face cream, designer sunglasses, French swimsuit and French towel which says 'soleil'. My friend Irene emails me every sunny day to say, 'Beach in 15 mins'. Fifteen minutes? Who's she kidding? This is Irene's look: no make-up, board shorts, short kind of bra top, jandals, old towel. Anyone would think it was casual Friday or something.

This is why keeping up appearances costs me a fortune in time and money

- Face cream applied in an upward movement every day since I turned thirteen.
- Body cream slathered on all over to stop from looking like a snake.
- Special toothpaste applied to stop teeth from rotting right out of my head.
- Face pack once a week because God only knows what will happen if there's a dead skin cell anywhere.
- Special lip cream to prevent chapping.
- Oil for the bath.
- Hard glove to exfoliate all over every day.
- Expensive shampoo and conditioner because cheap doesn't work.
- Shaving legs once a week.

- Toe-nail polish once a week.
- Plucking eyebrows once a week so as to not be channelling Frida Kahlo.
- Make-up – ranges from lipstick only to the full monty.
- Botox once every four months so my eyebrows go back to where God intended them, not where nature has mistakenly placed them.
- Dental work every six months so I won't have to put my teeth in a jar at night.
- Hair salon to dye my hair the colour red, which is the colour hair I know I should have been born with.
- HRT so I don't rip someone's throat out with my bare teeth when they annoy me.
- Thyroxine so I can stay awake all day and not become bovine.

Other women do a lot more than this: pedicures, facials, facelifts, liposuction, exercise, diets, manicures, spas, Brazilians, tummy tucks, tattooing, fillers. All this buying time, buying hope. If we stopped for one minute, we would not rot away right in front of people's eyes. If you want to know what happens if you don't do all this stuff and spend all this money and slap litres of body cream on, have a look at someone in a rest home who has lost their mind. Because they are too ill to remember how to look after themselves, their skin is scaly and sallow, their hair grey, the moustache is growing, the lines on the face are deep, the eyebrows are shaggy. The thing is, we were never meant to live this long. Medieval folk never had to worry about dry skin, uneven hair colour, or any diseases of ageing for that matter – they didn't last long enough. No peasant in ancient Egypt ever said, 'God I just can't stand my flabby arms' or 'Arthur, I think I'm having a stroke.' So now we live too long.

Occasionally, body cells don't die as they are programmed to and make a mistake – they start dividing and proliferating wildly, and this is called cancer. It cannot be caused or prevented by what you eat; in fact no one really knows why it happens. Normally billions of cells die every day by breaking down and devouring themselves. Other cells clean up the mess. As it happens, cells make the dividing mistake regularly but the body has elaborate mechanisms for dealing with it. I know it seems like cancer is everywhere, but in fact humans suffer one fatal malignancy for each 100 million billion cell divisions. Lots of unwanted chemicals enter our bodies all the time. Most leave quickly, but some stay – asbestos and silica in the lungs, dioxins in our blood, et cetera. The key word is *dose*. People who die of 'old age' have died of either cancer or heart failure because the body has just worn out. Strangely enough, given how much money we spend on creams, nobody has ever died of unmoisturised skin.

Going pewter

People have been dyeing their hair or wearing wigs for centuries, on and off. The Neanderthals coloured both their hair and their bodies and later so did the Saxons. This was not to look hot on Saturday night – it was to denote social or political position and scare off adversaries. Cleopatra used henna, as did lots of Egyptians. As mentioned in the 'Why Redheads Have More Fun' essay, naturally red hair appeared in the 1500s as a genetic mutation and had two results. People either punished natural redheads as the colour was thought to be the work of the devil, or they copied it. Then when Queen Elizabeth came on the scene with natural fiery red hair, everyone wanted it. They painted their faces white to dramatise the hair colour. In the 1700s, folk wore powdered wigs of all colours – yellow, white, pink, blue. Women bleached their hair blonde with caustic soda and darkened it with silver nitrate. Cripes! In 1867 it was discovered that hydrogen peroxide would bleach hair blonde, but it wasn't really till the 1950s that every harlot in existence went 'bottle blonde'. It was basically in the year I was born, 1949, that women all over the world started dyeing their hair, both in salons and at home, and these days it is guessed that 75 per cent of women dye their hair. Safe hair dye meant you could lie – you could pretend to be young. You weren't doing it to scare the enemy; you weren't doing it to have a laugh; you were doing it to trick yourself and everyone else into believing you were something you were not.

There comes a moment in every woman's life where she notices little silver linings on the perfect clouds of her hair. It usually happens in her thirties, but in my case it started when I was seventeen. Believe it or not I accepted and ignored it till I was in my early forties. Till then I had never put any dye in my hair, ever. It was only when someone mistook one of my sisters for my daughter that I *had* to take action. I went straight to the red dye pot and stayed there. Some of my friends have stopped dyeing and gone to pewter, and I have considered it many times but can't quite do it. It seems to me it depends on your complexion, the shade of pewter your hair goes naturally and the style in which your hair is cut. Also, certain professions permit pewter more than others; for example you would never see a grey-haired newsreader, but you would see a silver-fox editor. The more artistic or intelligent you are, the less likely you are to dye your hair. Most people who do, dye it the wrong, unflattering colour and have the wrong cut. Hairdressers should be shot for the inappropriate colour they put on older women's hair. Also, the price of hair colouring is scandalous – a completely inflated price based on buying hope. My friend Colleen dyed her hair dark red for a long time then got sick of it and went to her natural silver. It is absolutely stunning, suits her much better and has actually improved her looks – she looks like Marilyn Monroe now. Okay, so she's beautiful anyway, but her red hair did her no favours.

The wisdom is that if you are going to let your hair go pewter, you usually need to go short, sassy and strong, and to have your hair cut and styled frequently. You can't be looking like someone from Greenpeace, who's more interested in whales than looking good. You have to be making a statement. And you would save yourself a fortune, which could be spent on shoes. Author Anne Kreamer, who wrote *Going Gray*, maintains that a whole generation got tricked into believing dyed hair makes you look younger. She says that when she finally transitioned to her natural pewter, she felt empowered and relieved she was no longer masking her real self – also surprised at how good she looked and how happy it made her.

What happens to female health decade by decade

Teens
Up until twenty, bar eczema, the inability to communicate except by screaming, excessive marinating in not only oestrogen but also progesterone and testosterone, and feeling that no one understands her, it's pretty plain sailing health-wise. Teenage indulgences such as smoking, drinking, drugging, eating complete and utter rubbish, self-inflicted sporting injuries and treating boys as aliens will eventually put future health at risk.

Twenties

The twenties start showing the stresses of risk-taking, smoking and multiple sexual partners. Sexual diseases are a risk, as is cervical cancer and the beginnings of osteoporosis. She will need counselling from a psychologist or 300 of her closest friends when her heart is properly broken for the first time. Her brain changes every day (a whopping 25 per cent every month) due to the influence of above-mentioned hormones. This is the time of the first marriage, first child and first serious job. She is holding a lot of balls up in the air.

Thirties

In her thirties, because of her twenties, the female has the beginnings of not only cervical cancer but also lymphoma, cardiovascular disease, heart disease, high blood pressure and a few thousand dead brain cells thanks to all those joints she smoked in her twenties. Her 'mummy brain' is calmed by progesterone, which prevents her from strangling her children. She has less interest in sex if she has children, but more if she is single. This doesn't stop her from getting pregnant again. She is still holding a lot of balls up in the air.

Forties

If she hasn't given up the fags, she may have the beginnings of lung disease, but this is much more common among men. Now is the danger time for breast cancer, diabetes, thyroid problems and heart disease (the number one killer of women). For the first time in her life, she has to think about diet and exercise – the weight starts going up for no apparent reason. It is very hard for her to accept that she must change her ways. She might get pregnant again and is still juggling all those balls.

Fifties

Because of all that red meat and fat and not enough vegetables, the fabulous fifties herald colon and lung cancer. Heart attacks drop out of the sky; she can't read a thing without glasses and the beginnings of impotence in her mate starts to drive her crazy, especially when he turns to mad things like Viagra. Perimenopause starts, if it has not already started at forty-five. Oestrogen and progesterone begin slowly leaching away, causing mood swings, sleeplessness, hot flushes and dry skin. She continues to put on weight and considers buying a gun to deal with people who annoy her.

Sixties

Dementia can start in the sixties. If her husband suddenly starts to be very patient and treat her kindly like a mental patient, it is because she is no longer playing with a full deck. Ovarian and uterine cancers become a risk, as does osteoporosis – things like bones start breaking. Cholesterol problems ensure she can't enjoy fat on her meat and yolks in her omelettes (neither of which actually have any connection with cholesterol). She will never be bothered by hormonal swings again because menopause is over, hormones are over, everything settles down.

Seventies and beyond

Cancer becomes more and more of a risk, especially leukaemia and vaginal cancer. From seventy on, life can't get any worse and she finally chooses easier sports, like golf and line dancing, accepts the hair, hearing, eyesight situation, and starts enjoying herself again. She has nothing to lose, so develops a relationship with her doctor who turns out to be quite interesting, because he's from some exotic country she's never heard of. She gets things fixed when they go wrong and thanks God she's alive. Women last much longer than men generally so she will probably be widowed.

Gourmandise

It is unbelievably difficult to have to care about how much you eat. We all know how it works – you eat what you want till you're full then you do it again at lunch time then you do it again at dinner. You have done this all your life and you've always been a normal weight for your height and age. And then one day, without changing anything, you're not. The horrible, wicked thing is that you *have* changed something – you are older and you have hormonal changes and you don't need as much food. That's the simple fact of it. So you are faced with the ghastly proposition of limiting the one thing that gives you the most pleasure the most often. And then, as if that isn't boring enough, you have to find the clothes that go with this changing body shape. Dressing inappropriately for your age and shape is not only an external problem – it is also internal. You need to find out why you can't let go of being in your twenties. It is very hard to accept, especially if you were beautiful and relied on attention and compliments to feel good. A therapist would probably get you to make two lists: the good things and the bad things about being twenty, thirty, forty, et cetera. Wearing young clothes doesn't make you look young – it makes you look tragic and lost and strangers start feeling sorry for you. If you are wearing clothes from another era in your life it doesn't just mean you're out of fashion, because who cares, it means you haven't gone on to the next wonderful stage in your life. You are different in your thirties, forties and fifties – your hair changes colour, your body changes shape, you are different inside and none of it is bad. It is just different. Well okay . . . so it's pretty bad.

• • •

As you get older you're supposed to know everything about wine and impress people at dinner parties with your sparkling conversation about sauvignon blanc – the most overrated grape in the world. Wine is very good for you, so you should drink a couple of glasses daily as part of a healthy diet. Personally, I like whiskey. Whiskey's like glue – it makes you bond with people and you need all the bonding action you can get as time goes by.

Going to my mother's homeland of Ireland really increased my whiskey knowledge, as they are really mad for it. I willingly went to workshops on distillation, maturation and blending. I've always been fascinated by the changes a spirit undergoes, simply by the mere action of putting it in a wooden barrel and walking away for a few years, so I found myself in the presence of angels and experts in casks and maturation. Ageing whiskey in wood is almost like a fourth distillation, because the spirit is further purified over time. Eighty per cent of whiskey's flavour results from maturation, and in Ireland they always use oak casks that have held other alcoholic beverages because (a) new wood will overpower an Irish whiskey and (b) the port, sherry and bourbon casks impart a delicious flavour in the magical process that goes on in the darkness of the barrels.

As it warms and expands, the whiskey pushes into the wood and a whopping 2 to 3 per cent evaporates every year. This is called the 'angel's share'. Maturation happens in fits and starts and is also affected by weather, strangely. The cask breathes like a lung, you know, and when the temperature drops, the alcohol 'contracts', leaching extracts from the wood. When you're tasting a whiskey you taste it in a wine glass, usually cut with water. A good one is toffee-sweet on the nose and full of spice and sherry-impregnated wood, with a gorgeous mellow, lingering taste. I used never to put water in my whiskey after childhood because I thought why would you spend twelve years getting all the water out, then add water, but all the experts assured me that anyone who knows what they're doing adds a third of water to open up a good whiskey. I have it on excellent authority that you can cut that water down to a quarter as you age. Whiskey drinking helps prevent cancer even more than red wine drinking does – it's the powerful antioxidants and free-radical scavengers in the ellagic acid – but you have to drink single malts.

Things I would have done differently

- I would never have lied so much as a child, because by the time I realised it was getting very complicated to keep up with, no one knew who I was any more.
- I should not have called all those men male-ego-testicle-imperial-pig-dogs – one adjective would've been enough.
- The patchwork crushed-velvet bellbottoms I made on my sewing machine when I was twenty-two – how could I possibly have thought that would be a look? I know it was the 1970s and I was stoned, but still . . .
- I wish I had known my looks would improve with age and been less envious of beautiful women. Now with modern technology everyone looks the same, liberating us to reveal the beautiful person inside. Or not.
- I should've gone into therapy when I was six – it would have been cheaper.

- If I had known that the fat bit around my middle at forty-five was still going to be there at sixty I would have eaten more, because it turns out the body is a temple with curved walls.
- I'm sorry to every wait-person I didn't tip in my life – what goes round comes round.
- I wish I had understood that secrecy in relationships, like fear, is a lonely and cancerous path.
- It's never too early in the day to start drinking if you find someone who's not you in your boyfriend's bed.
- All families are dysfunctional. No? So name one.
- I was never going to make good pastry from wholemeal flour and brown rice was never going to be palatable – it was just never going to happen. And all those mung beans didn't change a thing. My father (who's hitting ninety) was right – the secret to a long life is whiskey, no exercise, cake and cigars.
- I wouldn't have brought home all those Mexican ponchos, Bolivian skirts, Vietnamese ao dais, Spanish flamenco dresses. I would have put them in the bin at the airport.
- I would've had a dog, because then when I slammed the door on those men I wouldn't have been alone in the house. At least a dog is grateful and licks your hand, even if it is only because you are feeding him. No man ever licked my hand.

- In terms of interior decor, I should have stuck to white. I'm not Mexican. I didn't really need yellow, brown, pink, blue walls.
- I didn't know the difference between mahogany and monogamy. I should have stuck to mahogany, but it was hard to see the forest for the trees.
- I would've understood that time passes.

● ● ●

Of course now that I'm older, I'm sagacious, full of insight, gracious and melodious in my outlook. I understand completely what is important in life. I know that just around the corner are calmness, maturity, spiritual awakening and patience. I am becoming my true self. But can we talk? I cannot accept my arms. I'm just going out to buy one more jar of hope.

How to Control the Universe with Egg Whites

Nothing is more rewarding than bending
the universe to your will in an exercise that
is both basic and extravagant.

Peta Mathias

Beating egg whites till they're stiff is a metaphor for life
– just when you thought your existence would never be
more than flaccid transparent snot, something happens
to turn it into tight white light. In terms of the egg white,
that something was as simple as movement and air.
When life gets tough, change the recipe, move around
both physically and emotionally, and keep breathing out.
Anyone can breathe in. An egg is a complete food source
which, amazingly, is given to us by birds. It is also a very
beautiful, sensual shape.

We've all had run-ins with eggs – soufflés that went nowhere, omelettes with no yolks because some mad doctors told us it would help our cholesterol, and soft-boiled ova, where the white looks like something that seeps out of a mucous membrane. And then there's the significant other who in spite of years of obedience training, insists on crowding you, the expert egg-cooker, as you work. According to exotic animal trainers you can teach a hyena to pirouette and an elephant to paint, so you should be able to teach a partner to stop interfering while you're going about perfecting something in the kitchen. Here's how to deal with the irritating, interfering partner: place a bowl of fried bacon on the other side of the room. The exotic animal, your partner, will crawl on his belly to the bacon because no one, including vegetarians, can resist fried salty pig fat. While they are distracted, enjoy your calm space in the kitchen, cooking the omelette. Now serve it to grateful partner, who will swoon at the primal feast of eggs and butter that you have seen fit to place before him. See how you can control your universe with eggs?

● ● ●

Delia Smith has written extensively on how to boil an egg, so no one could ever say of a woman again: 'She can't even boil an egg.' An egg white is mostly water, but also contains 10 per cent protein and a small amount of fat and ash. It is a colourless liquid when raw, that turns white when beaten till stiff or cooked. When heated, the protein starts to coagulate at 60°C. When the yolk is heated it firms up and sets more slowly than the white, which is why it's possible to have a runny yolk with a set white when you cook an egg. When making omelettes, some folk beat the whites separately, then the yolks, then fold them in together. This is the work of the devil and only marginally less criminal than making omelettes out of egg whites only. Thank goodness we're allowed to eat whole eggs again. The Eggpire strikes back and the dark days are over, except for those who truly do not enjoy eating.

Egg whites not only changed history in the culinary domain, but medieval doctors applied them to seal and treat wounds and broken bones. Egg whites were also used to make glue, photographic paper and, till the sixteenth century, as a fixer or binder with coloured, water-soluble pigments for painting. Called tempera, it was brilliant because it would mix with anything – pigment, gold, silver, chalk – dried quickly and lasted for ages, retaining colour for centuries. It was brushed on to the canvas in a sort of feathering technique in very fine, light layers. It also gave a lovely patina, which is still used today in some types of painting, for example Russian icons. If you have a hankering to paint a good forgery of *The Last Supper*, you beat egg white till stiff, leave it overnight then brush it on your painting to make it look old. If you have nothing else to do. Egg whites are also used in porn films to simulate ejaculate. If you have nothing else to do.

Separation anxiety

Some people think separating eggs means putting the brown ones on one side of the bench and the white ones on the other. What it really means is that you have to get the whites away from the yellows – but only after you have completed your science degree. This process alone is enough to give you pre-traumatic stress syndrome. It works better if you have fresh, room-temperature eggs. The older the egg is, the more likely the yolk is to break as its covering membrane is thinner. If an egg is straight from the fridge, it is harder for the proteins to unfold and let the air in while you beat.

On the subject of fresh eggs, when I was in Cork I discovered something I had never seen before at the English Market on Grand Parade. Stacked up among the hand-churned farm butter, buttermilk, milk with the cream on top (something from my childhood that you very rarely see now), raw milk cheeses and soda bread, were trays upon trays of shiny buttered eggs. As soon as the eggs are laid and while the shells are still relatively soft, they are dipped in hot butter. This preserves them longer – for up to six months – and gives the eggs a creamy taste. This preservation technique was created originally to ensure a winter supply of eggs when the hens were not laying a lot. In fact, big egg companies still do a version of that by dipping eggs in a very fine oil to keep them fresh.

Right, so said egg is in your hand. The doctor and the priest are on standby. You've got your pinny on. The stars are in alignment. There are several ways of proceeding. Most people tap the eggshell gently on the side of a bowl or with a knife, whereupon a small crack appears. From this crack you break the shell into two halves and, letting the white dribble out into the bowl, tip the yolk from shell to shell till all the white has gone. You are left with a perfectly round yellow ball of deliciousness in the shell. If you have let a bit of yolk fall into the whites, you have to discard the whole lot or use it for something else, like smearing all over your face in a face mask. If you are not very practised at this, do the egg cracking and separating over another bowl, separate from the one you already have egg whites in – this way you lower the risk of yolk contamination.

Another way of separating eggs is to crack the shell over a bowl then pour the egg into your hand, letting the white slip down through your fingers. Some people crack the egg into a saucer, cover the yolk with an egg cup and pour the white off. You can buy an apparatus called an egg-separator, but surely you're not that challenged. By the way, if it's yolks you're after, a bit of white doesn't matter at all. If you are not going to use the whites immediately, you can refrigerate them for two days at most, but allow them to come back to room temperature before beating.

They can also be frozen. Yolks can be kept in the fridge for a few days but don't freeze very successfully. An egg white is about two tablespoons, so a good idea is to freeze them in ice trays; then you know exactly how many you have. If you freeze them together in a container, label the container with the number of whites it contains, otherwise you will go back to that mental breakdown state trying to chip off what you think might be six eggs' worth. I never keep egg whites for a rainy day because I know the war is over. My friends are scandalised by this profligate behaviour, but I will not be rehabilitated because I know exactly what will happen to those egg whites – they will stay in the back of the fridge till I throw them out. The back of the fridge is where egg whites go to die.

Beat till stiff

Why do runny egg whites turn to foam when beaten? When you whisk them, the egg white liquid is drawn through itself, making the protein molecules separate and disorientate. The other thing that makes proteins unfold is the mixing-in of air that occurs. This disturbing of the natural state of the proteins is called denaturation. The proteins rush to be together where the water and air meet, then clump with other unfolded proteins. This creates foam and the air is held in. Miraculously, this beating process expands the egg whites up to eight times their original volume. Lots can go wrong when you're trying to beat an egg white till stiff and keep it like that, so the trick is to stabilise it, and one way is to use a copper or silver mixing bowl. The metal in the bowl helps to bind the proteins more tightly. The bowl must be scrupulously clean, and the best way to ensure this is to rub a cut lemon around it. You can use glass and ceramic bowls, of course, and it is helpful if you throw in a little powdered copper. You can also add a little salt, lemon juice or cream of tartar. Acid changes the pH of the egg whites, increasing the hydrogen and stabilising the proteins. Any suggestion of oil or fat will prevent the proteins from denaturing, which is why you can't let even the tiniest smear of egg yolk get in. The beater you use – which can be two forks held back to back, a birch whisk, balloon whisk, electric hand beater or food processor – must be very clean. I mean, you can see how easy it would be to have a mental breakdown over this, never mind that you'll never get a husband out of it. People talk about the stress of driving in downtown traffic – they've obviously never tried to beat egg whites till stiff.

When I was a chef in Paris, I was taught how to beat egg whites with a large, stainless steel balloon whisk in a figure of eight motion. This is a very efficient way of beating and with practice you can get very fast at it – even turn it into a party trick. The thing with cooking techniques is you have to prove you are at the top of your game – it's relentless: professional kitchens are Armageddons of competitiveness, believe me. Not many cooks can pull off the figure of eight coup in company, so by performing it at a party you are way ahead of any pretenders to the throne of exhibitionism. These days I prefer an electric hand beater because it is less tiring and you can clearly see what you are doing. If you are using a hand whisk or old-fashioned rotary egg beater (the one you hold in one hand and turn with the other), you must start at a slow speed then increase it and keep up a good pace. It's not a good idea to wander off for a sherry in the middle of it. Depending on the recipe, egg whites can be beaten till they hold *soft peaks* – a tight white foam which can ribbon and peak but won't stay like that if you don't bake it immediately; *firm peaks* – a firm, smooth foam which forms a peak that curls at the point; or *stiff peaks* – a very firm, shiny concoction that will hold to the point where you can actually slice it.

Birch whisk

These are the original egg and sauce beaters and are made from bunches of stiff birch twigs tied together at one end. They can also be made from stiff straw, juniper and black-currant twigs. They date back to the sixteenth century and are still in use – you can buy them in kitchenware shops. They serve a very real purpose for dedicated cooks as they are absolutely the best thing to whip a béchamel or hollandaise sauce with, due to their flexibility. A birch whisk can get into all the corners of the pot that a balloon whisk can't. They are pretty and easy to work with – I use mine quite a lot, but they are not particularly effective for egg whites.

I'm sorry to bring this up, but those naughty Swedes and Finns also use birch whisks in the sauna. The difference is the leaves are left on and the branches tied with the underside in (they can be young oak, lime tree or eucalyptus). You can use them fresh or dried, dipped in water. The Finns and Swedes lightly beat themselves with the whisk to exfoliate, enhance blood circulation, massage muscles, open pores, sweat and relax (the fragrance being wonderful). I know what you're thinking, so I'll move on to the regular non-flagellation whisk.

Whisk

Modern whisks, called sauce whisks or French whisks, are generally made from plastic, metal, nylon or wire, and the best seem to be the silicone-coated wire ones as they have more wires and are non-stick. The curved, tear-drop-shaped tines (prongs) are joined at the handle and it was the darling Julia Child who made them popular in America. Hopeless in a Swedish sauna.

Rotary hand beater

The adorable rotary hand beater was invented in 1856 and originally made from cast iron or tin. The very first one had only one whisk. Some of them were very beautiful with all sorts of particulars like heart-shaped dashers (beaters), ribbon-design dashers, ornate turning wheels, handles and knobs, twisted wire handles, double propellers. There was one designed that even had a funnel attached to it for when you were making mayonnaise so the oil could go into the mixture drop by drop – I think this is brilliant. Some could be table mounted or had a tin bottom stand so the beater could stand up straight on its own in the bowl or on the bench. The modern versions are about 23 cm tall, have a handle at the top, a crankshaft in the middle and blunt blades at the bottom. The main problem is that you need two hands to operate it. How the blades work is that one goes clockwise and the other one goes counter-clockwise.

Electric beater

Believe it or not the first electric beater came into being as early as 1885 in the United States. It was rather cumbersome, with the adjustable motor sitting on an iron stand on the side. An electric beater follows the same principle as a rotary beater but with electricity so no effort is involved. You can have a hand-held one, or a bowl on a fixed stand wherein the beaters not only go around each other but also around the bowl. Electric beaters are particularly wonderful if you're making a long-winded meringue, adding the sugar in nanogram by nanogram.

A mark of expertise

'Beat till stiff' was a term I grew up with, intoned in every cookbook, cooking lesson and baking adventure, and to perform it successfully was proof of expertise. It was made clear to us that if you can't beat egg whites properly, you may as well go jump in the lake because you'll be no use to any husband. If you can't bake a meringue, you may as well not even walk out of the house; but then there are lots of reasons to not leave the house, most of them associated with personal appearance. There are certain things that matter in this valley of tears – lipstick is one, a properly denatured lump of albumen is another, getting your leg over on Sunday . . . I could go on . . . You see, so many extraordinary things can be done with a stiff egg white and most of them happen in a kitchen, that seat of all happiness and magic.

In the ghastly misery of childhood where one controls absolutely nothing about one's little life because one is only seven, the earthy craving to eat and cook was born in me. I could watch my calm grandmother cooking for hours, almost drugged with the smells, the beating of things which turned them into something else, the taste of raw pastry, uncooked meringue mixture, fish cake paste. If she turned her back I would put my hand into anything I could and eat it. Being in a kitchen was like being in a sauna saturated with perfumes and aromas where only good reigned. But it was also solid and safe and fecund at the same time, as if permeated by woman hormones. I didn't really aspire to beat egg whites till perfectly stiff because I cared about a perfect meringue; I aspired to my grandmother's perfectness and kindness (which I never achieved), thus attaining happiness.

You can clarify consommé, wine and Champagne with egg whites. There are glorious inventions like pavlova, named for the Russian ballerina Anna Pavlova. A New Zealand hotel chef whipped it together for her 1926 tour by making a large round meringue and topping it with whipped cream and fruit like strawberries and passionfruit. Macaroons, beloved of food fashionistas and beauty addicts, are little baked rounds of egg white, almond meal and sugar flavoured with perfumes such as lemon, violet, gooseberry and green tea. Two rounds are stuck together with ganache, jam or buttercream (also made with beaten egg whites). The French claim them, but the real origin is probably Italy and the best ones are made in Paris by Pierre Hermé. Unlike a meringue, macarons literally melt in your mouth and you can eat as many of them as you like in the interests of continuing masticatory pleasure.

Another fashionable and lovely egg white, almond meal, butter, sugar and flour concoction is what in Australia and New Zealand is called a friand. Friands are baked in an oval shape, are deliciously sticky and often baked with a bit of fruit on top such as raspberries, Black Doris plums, rhubarb or lemon. Sometimes they are made with other nut meals such as hazelnut. When you ask for a sweet friand in France they don't know what you're talking about, as a French friand is a sausage roll. A celestial dacquoise is a layered cake of hazelnut and almond meringue and buttercream. One of my favourite and oft-made egg white desserts is the Italian semifreddo (half cold) – a non-churned type of ice cream. You separately beat egg yolks, egg whites, cream and flavourings like pistachio and marsala, then fold them all together before freezing. The egg white story is endless – how can we forget nougat, madeleines, marshmallows, marzipan, floating islands and génoise sponge? How can we sleep at night thinking of these voluptuous things?

Meringue

The most famous reason you would ever beat an egg white till stiff is the justly feared meringue – that noble method of eating sugar held together by clouds of whipped albumen. The word meringue is French, but possibly originated from German and was first seen in 1691. Meringue-like confections were made before this but not with this name. It was only in the sixteenth century that French cooks figured out that if you beat egg whites with a birch whisk, they turn into foam. Enchanted with this discovery, they folded this foam in with beaten cream and called it snow, but obviously it wasn't going to stay stable for long and also, you couldn't bake with it. So how to keep the egg whites stiff? The answer is to beat in sugar. But it couldn't be coarse sugar – it had to be very, very fine and light and it had to be beaten in slowly and patiently, otherwise you would get collapse or the old weeping problem, where the moisture from too many fat grains of sugar added too quickly produces syrup. This confection of stiff egg white and sugar was originally called sugar puff in England, then imported the more glamorous name 'meringue' from France. Beguilingly, they whipped caraway seeds into it. Tiny individual meringues were made as snacks and bigger ones were broken in half and filled with whipped cream. It was always difficult to make a large meringue, but in the eighteenth century the vacherin dessert was invented where it didn't really matter if the meringue wasn't high or properly cooked in the centre, because you cooked two flattish rings then layered them with berries and whipped cream. The vacherin is so-called because it resembles the shape, colour and rich creaminess of a vacherin cheese.

The basic method of adding the sugar is this: beat egg whites till foamy on a slow speed then add a little salt or cream of tartar. Continue beating faster till stiff. Now, reducing the speed, add the caster sugar literally one tablespoon at a time till you have incorporated about a quarter of it. Make sure you wait till the sugar has been well mixed in before adding more. Keep adding sugar gradually till two-thirds of it is in. At this point you are now safe and you can keep beating the rest of the sugar in or fold it in with a spoon. You may wish to add a little vanilla. Some people actually keep beating for another five to fifteen minutes on a slow speed. Pipe or spoon the meringues immediately onto baking paper on an oven tray. Because a meringue is so light and so full of sugar it attracts heat and burns easily, so must be cooked, or really dried, at a very low temperature. What happens when you bake a meringue is that the mild heat causes the tiny air bubbles you have whipped in to expand, and this holds the denatured proteins firmly around them.

Place meringues in an oven preheated to 100°C and bake for one hour. Go sit in the garden, listen to the birds and drink pink champagne. Check the meringues halfway through by looking through the glass door; if they are looking even slightly coloured, turn the oven down to 70°C. If you have an Aga-type cooker you can even leave them in overnight at the lowest setting. Traditionally, meringues should be slightly crisp outside, dry and slightly gummy inside and still white in colour. When you gently tap them on the underside they should sound hollow. If you wanted to make thirty little meringues you would use four egg whites and 250 g of caster sugar. You could possibly add a little cornflour and a little baking powder. Keep them in a cake tin and only put icings or fillings in at the last minute.

Meringue is easier to make in the dry, cold winter because the summer heat and humidity destabilises it.

There are three types of meringue. *French meringue* is the easiest and most delicate, in which you just beat sugar and egg white till stiff then use immediately. You make dishes like oeufs à la neige, soufflés and little piped things. *Italian meringue* is what chefs use and is the most stable and trustworthy – they can make it in advance and it won't collapse. They pour boiling sugar syrup into beaten egg whites and keep beating till cool. The heat from the syrup makes the egg white proteins expand, almost like baking them. This type of meringue is normally the structure for something else like a complicated dessert, but is also good for tart toppings, icings, some ice creams and sorbets. *Swiss meringue* or cooked meringue is the hardest to make. A pastry chef will use the Italian method and whisk it over a pot of hot water. It's quite labour-intensive, but very stable and is used to make nougat glacé, cassata and buttercreams. There are variations of the meringue, such as the japonaise, made with ground almonds. In his cookbook *French*, Damien Pignolet gives the Viennese recipe for meringues flavoured with lime zest and chopped walnuts, then dusted with cocoa.

Chocolate mousse

This is one of the world's favourite desserts and when I die I want to go to a great big gastronomic brothel in the sky where I can have men covered in chocolate mousse. I first heard of mousse au chocolat when I moved to France in 1980 and ate it in a restaurant where it was placed on the table in a huge bowl and you just took as much as you liked. Chocolate mousse (meaning foam) is French and, believe it or not, was invented by the painter Henri de Toulouse-Lautrec. Prior to that the mousse technique had only been used for vegetables and fish. Toulouse-Lautrec loved hosting debauched parties in his Paris apartment and often treated his friends to provocative and decadent culinary and alcoholic experiments; one of his famous cocktails was 50/50 absinthe and cognac with a bit of ice. Any ordinary person would have a nosebleed even thinking about that. On a blissful and intoxicated evening, Toulouse-Lautrec did one of the most famous things in French gastronomy – mixed chocolate into a mousse.

The French adore anything with chocolate in it and life is just something that happens till you can get your next chocolate fix. In my restaurant in Paris, this dessert became the main point of people's lives in the 5th arrondissement. I made it with 70 per cent cocoa chocolate, sugar, a little fresh orange juice and rind, Grand Marnier and more egg whites than yolks. Sometimes I added vanilla, aniseed or freshly ground nutmeg. No cream. The original French recipe has only chocolate, butter, sugar and eggs. During the time I had my restaurant in Paris I went mad from overwork and stress, my weight evaporated to 55 kilos and I ate only chocolate and drank only red wine – that was my demented diet. Chocolate, of course, is well documented as a tonic to replace orgasms, alleviate bad humour, feed the intellect and cure a broken heart. Chocolate mousse is basically an antidepressant, so the more you let slide along your tongue, the better you feel. And egg whites have protein – how can that be bad?

Soufflé

In my restaurant in Paris I not only made chocolate mousse, I also made cheese soufflés till they were coming out my wazoo. You have to have a very hot oven to cook soufflés, so you can imagine that permanent heat in a small kitchen from an oven which had to be kept scorching throughout the whole service. I got to the point where they were fail-proof and desperately glamorous, unlike myself. The French word soufflé means puff or breath to describe the ephemeral lightness and airiness of this famous dish, invented in the seventeenth century by chef Beauvilliers. You make a savoury soufflé by folding grated cheese, crab or asparagus or whatever into a roux (flour and butter sauce). Then you stir egg yolks into that. Beat egg whites till stiff and fold them into everything else. The mixture is placed in buttered, high-sided ceramic soufflé dishes to three-quarters of the way up and baked in a bain-marie (water bath) in a hot oven for exactly the right amount of time (usually between 15 and 20 minutes). The number of minutes depends on the size of the soufflé dish. The mixture may be prepared and placed in the cooking dishes in advance and kept in the fridge. When you are ready to bake them they can go straight from the fridge to the oven. You cannot open the oven door during cooking, and your guests must already be seated at the table gasping with anticipation and not wandering around free-range, engaging in idle chatter. It is served and eaten immediately. In my restaurant I *always* used a bain-marie to ensure even and non-violent heat.

If a soufflé collapses it is because it is uncooked in the centre or has sat around too long before eating. If it doesn't rise in the first place it is usually because the oven isn't hot enough. Sometimes a soufflé will rise on an angle, which is a problem for control freaks. This usually happens in a fan oven, so try turning the convection fan off. One resolution to the terror of a fallen soufflé and resulting social exclusion is the method of twice-cooking. This seems desperately innovative but has actually been around for over a hundred years. You bake the soufflé as normal, let it cool then put it aside or in the fridge till you are going to serve it. Place it upended in a shallow baking dish, pour some cream over and re-cook it at a high heat, whereupon it will rise again. This is almost better than a regular soufflé because you get the delicious cooked cream. In 1965, Albert Roux of the famous London restaurant Le Gavroche invented the gloriously indulgent soufflé suissesse. In his method, he baked the soufflés in 8-cm tartlet tins in a very high oven for only three minutes, then upturned them into waiting shallow dishes of warmed, salted, double cream. They were sprinkled with grated Gruyère, returned to the oven for five minutes, then served.

You can also make divine sweet soufflés which are based on fruit purées or flavoured crème pâtissière or béchamel, folded in with a light French meringue. I used to make a soufflé Normand in my restaurant which involved Calvados-spiked crème pâtissière. Once made, diced macaroons and apples were stirred in, then the beaten egg whites folded in. You paint the soufflé dishes with melted butter then dust with caster sugar and place in the fridge till you are ready to cook. Fill the dishes up to the top with the sweet soufflé and even the surface off with a knife. A good chef's trick to make sure it rises evenly is to cut a shallow ring around the rim of the soufflé with the tip of the knife. There are endless sweet soufflés – Valrhona chocolate, Kir Royale (champagne and redcurrants), prune and Armagnac, passionfruit and praline, raspberry and amaretti.

Eating a good soufflé is like coating your palate with ambrosial moonbeams; and in the recipe for happy living, we need all the moonbeams we can lay our hands on.

Baked Alaska

Not many people make the endangered and preposterous baked (or bombe) Alaska these days but it used to be a very popular restaurant dish, God knows why. It was invented by an American restaurant in 1876 to celebrate

Alaska joining the United States. We all *know* who comes from Alaska, so preposterous seems to be something they specialise in. The truth is that it was stolen from the French, who thought it up long before. You make it by layering Grand-Marnier-spiked sponge cake, ice cream, sponge cake, ice cream, sponge cake, then slathering the whole lot with Swiss meringue. You bake it in a hot oven for a few minutes till golden, then serve it very quickly before the ice cream starts to melt. The point of it is the supposedly interesting juxtaposition of hot and cold and soft and creamy textures in your mouth. A relatively foolproof trick is to freeze the ice cream and sponge concoction till you are ready to bake it, then apply the meringue and glaze it with a culinary blow torch. I say 'relatively' because who wants freezing sponge going down their gullet? Personally, I think it is the most ridiculous invention after the coffee-making alarm clock and to subject my taste buds to such an arrogant assault is more than I am prepared to do in the interest of international culinary relations.

Transformation

The important thing about all transformation is that when something like a beater passes through the recipe of your life and stirs things up, don't resist it – allow your proteins to be denatured, your emotions to be drawn through themselves, your molecules to become disorientated. In this way of living lies expansion – just like the egg white that multiplies in volume by eight when beaten. What will emerge is lightness and harmony, but don't forget to stabilise your state of white light – keep yourself clean as my mother would say, be vigilant and don't allow malignant influences to spoil your recipe. Nothing is more rewarding than bending the universe to your will in an exercise that is both basic and extravagant. Standing in that kitchen, entering into that magic realm where things change before your eyes, you personally can turn slimy albumen into perfect white foamy light. If you can do it with a boring old egg white, you can do it with the recipe of your life.

Bibliography

Why Redheads Have More Fun
Colour by Victoria Finlay, Sceptre (Great Britain), 2002
Le Petit Livre des Couleurs by Michel Pastoureau and
     Dominique Simonnet, Editions du Panama (Paris),
     2005

Channelling Edith
My Life by Edith Piaf, Penguin (England), 1992

Tattooed Lady
Magpie Hall by Rachael King, Vintage (Auckland), 2009
*Marks of Civilization: artistic transformations of the human
     body*, edited by Arnold Rubin, University of California,
     (Los Angeles), 1988
Ta Moko: the art of Maori tattoo by DR Simons, Reed
     (Auckland), 1986

How to Control the Universe with Egg Whites
French by Damien Pignolet, Lantern (Penguin) (Victoria,
     Australia), 2005
French Lessons by Justin North, Hardie Grant Books
     (Victoria, Australia), 2007
The Oxford Companion to Food by Alan Davidson, Oxford
     University Press (Oxford), 1999

Can we help it if we're Fabulous?

And other thoughts on being a woman

peta mathias

Can We Help it if We're Fabulous?

The irrepressible Peta Mathias is a woman who has never been afraid to embrace life with all its glorious inconsistencies, joys and heartbreaks. While we know her as an engaging television presenter, an inspiring food writer and a delightful raconteur, in *Can We Help it if We're Fabulous?* Peta instantly becomes every woman's confidante, as she shares with us the wisdom she has learnt over her years of living outrageously. She is a woman who appreciates the importance of a gorgeous pair of shoes and the perfect shade of lipstick. She knows the value of good friends, great music, lively conversation, beautiful surroundings and a one-way ticket to an exotic destination. And having loved and lost – more than once – Peta also has her own theories on why relationships begin and end. And then there's the sex chapter!

Inspirational, razor-witted and irresistibly funny, *Can We Help it if We're Fabulous?* is Peta Mathias at her wisest – and naughtiest. This book is for each and every fabulous woman out there.

Just in Time to be Too Late

In her bestselling guide to womanhood *Can We Help it if We're Fabulous?*, the irrepressible Peta Mathias shared with us her thoughts on being a woman. Now, in *Just in Time to be Too Late*, she turns her attention to what it means to be a man in the twenty-first century.

What makes men cry? Why are Bad Boys so irresistible? What exactly is the point of sport? To what extent is a man's self worth connected to his job? What do men look for in a relationship? Why do men lie? What does he need to be happy? And, of course, why are men like buses?

Though she has been married and has had her fair share of meaningful relationships and flirtatious dalliances, Peta is the first to admit that she knew very little about the opposite sex when she began work on this book – 'A virgin would know more about men than I do because she's probably listened more.'

Just in Time to be Too Late is a highly personal and frequently hilarious pilgrimage that will resonate with women everywhere.